LET ME ILLUSTRATE

Stories and Quotations for Christian Communicators

ALBERT P. STAUDERMAN

AUGSBURG Publishing House • Minneapolis

LET ME ILLUSTRATE

Library of Congress Catalog Card No. 83-70511
International Standard Book No. 0-8066-2017-X

Scripture quotations unless otherwise noted are from the Revised Standard Version of the Bible, copyright 1946, 1952, and 1971 by the Division of Christian Education of the National Council of Churches.

Manufactured in the United States of America

Dedicated to some 300 congregations—including Lutheran, Methodist, Disciples, Presbyterian, and Roman Catholic—whose response to my preaching encouraged me to compile this book; and especially to United Lutheran, Mount Vernon, New York; St. Paul's, Teaneck, New Jersey; St. John's, Melrose Park, Pennsylvania; and First Evangelical, West Palm Beach, Fla., in which I have held membership.

Contents

7	The Use of Illustrations	56	Everyday Religion
11	Illustrations	60	Example
12	Adversity	62	Excuses
16	Age	62	Faith and Doubt
16	Anxiety	67	Faith at Work
18	Art	69	Faithfulness
20	Attitude	70	False Hopes
22	Bible	71	Freedom
26	Books	73	Future
27	Brotherhood	74	Gardens
30	Change	75	Goals
32	Character	77	God's Love
34	Charity	79	God's Power
35	Children	82	God's Presence
36	Christian Religion	85	God's Promises
38	Christmas	86	Greed, Selfishness
40	Churches	88	Growth
42	Commitment	89	Guidance
45	Communications	91	Guilt, Forgiveness
46	Compassion	94	Happiness
47	Conscience	95	Hope
48	Contentment	97	Humility
50	Courage	100	Immortality
51	Creation	102	Indifference
53	Cross	104	Individuals
54	Decision	105	Influence

107	Integrity	145	Remembrance
111	Introductions and Invocations	146	Resources, Inner Strength
112	Labor	147	Rewards
113	Law and Justice	148	Science
114	Love	150	Service
114	Loyalty	153	Sheep and Shepherds
116	Marriage and Family	154	Sin
119	Mercy	155	Stewardship
120	Missions	160	Success
122	Modern Life	161	Teachers
124	Morality	162	Temptation
125	Mothers	163	Thanksgiving
126	Nation	165	Time
127	Opportunity	167	Unity
130	Patience	168	Vision
132	Peace	171	Witnessing
133	Power	173	Words
135	Prayer	175	World Affairs
138	Preaching	176	Worship
140	Pride	179	Writers and Writing
141	Progress	181	Index of Sources and Topics
142	Religion		

The Use of Illustrations

A speech, sermon, or article without illustrations is like a wall without windows. It may serve its purpose, but there's nothing beautiful or interesting about it, and it certainly does not let in much light. The word *illustration* itself comes from a Latin root which means "to light up" or "clarify."

Obviously any wall needs a sound structure. A teacher, preacher, writer, or speaker must have a message to convey and the facts to back it up. Factual presentations, however, are enhanced and embellished by the well-placed interjection of a lighter word, an applicable story, or a fitting quotation. Even a quip—a "one-liner"—can reduce the tension of concentration or boredom and help establish rapport between the communicator and the listener.

A reader who tires of plodding through a dull article can simply toss the magazine or book aside, perhaps to take it up at another time. Polite audiences listening to a speaker have less opportunity to escape. Caught in such a situation, they close their minds to what is being said (or turn off their hearing aids) and get lost in their own thoughts. When there is danger of this happening, an experienced speaker knows the need to jerk the audience back to attention by the use of an illustration or anecdote. It has the attention-getting quality needed to revive the flagging interest of one's hearers. When the speaker says, "That reminds me of . . ." or "For example . . . ," the hearer knows there will be a brief period of relief from the pressure of concentration. Their relaxed mood—if the story is good enough!—will make them more receptive to whatever follows, and the story itself may help implant the speaker's idea firmly in their minds.

For the same reasons creative writing courses advocate the "layer cake" method of developing an article. A layer cake consists of a solid section of baked dough with an enticing and tasty frosting on it. Sometimes several layers are piled up, separated and enriched by the delicious sugary frosting. Without frosting, most people would be disappointed in the layer cake. Good writers apply this layer cake principle in their writing.

Good illustrations, however, should not merely be bits of fluff to divert the attention of hearers or readers. If they distract from the main object of the presentation, they may do more harm than good. Their message needs to support and strengthen the theme of the presentation. This is particularly important since often the illustration or story remains in the mind of the hearer long after the rest of the presentation is forgotten.

When it is pertinent to the subject matter, an illustration or story can be inserted into a presentation at any transition point. Beware, however, lest your story becomes so long that by the time you end it, your audience has forgotten what you were saying when it started. Make sure also that your illustration or anecdote is sufficiently germane to the subject matter that you won't leave your audience wondering what the point of it was. Often illustrations can be adapted for a particular theme by the change of a few words. In any case, an illustration becomes more pertinent when you put it into your own words. A quotation, on the other hand, should always be faithful to the original words and not slanted or distorted to suit your theme!

Choosing the right illustration is important. It should apply both to the subject matter and to the mood of the moment. A humorous illustration that draws a laugh from the audience may be the best kind, if it relates to the subject. An extraneous joke simply thrown in for a laugh, however, may destroy the theme development the speaker is attempting to put across. In a church that I sometimes attend, an elderly retired pastor, who obviously is permitted some special liberties, assists in conducting the service and during the announcement period tells his "joke of the week." Even though the joke is often funny, it bears no relationship to the theme of the service and is, in my opinion, a needless distraction.

On the other hand, the expert telling of a story—even a biblical story—can be the most memorable part of a service. In some churches the minister calls the children together for a brief children's sermon, often in story form. Many a time I've remembered such a story far longer than the regular sermon. There are values in storytelling, in simplicity, and in brevity.

Story is an ancient and effective way of conveying information that remains in the minds of hearers. The first threads of human history came in the form of stories, handed down from generation to generation. The most memorable parts of the Old Testament are its stories. The gospel narratives are stories—true stories, but stories nevertheless. In Greece, Aesop presented a whole system of ethics in the form of fables or stories. History is just one long story, as the word itself suggests.

Many cultures had high esteem for their storytellers. Not only did they entertain, but they were effective teachers. Jesus knew the value of storytelling. His parables use story form to depict some important religious principles and truths. Never despise the use of a story, whether you are communicating with simple children or learned professors!

Here are some guidelines for choosing and using illustrations:

1. The illustration should reinforce what you have been saying and/or contribute to the forward flow of your thought.

2. The illustration should be believable; if it is farfetched it may cast doubts on the integrity of your entire presentation.

3. The illustration should not distract the audience from the major thrust of your presentation.

4. The illustration should have some intrinsic message of value, so that if the illustration is the only thing an audience remembers from your presentation it will still get your point across.

Illustrations in this book have been chosen with these guidelines in mind. Every effort has been made to locate the source and secure permission for use of copyrighted material. Inadvertent omissions called to the publisher's attention will be noted in future editions.

These illustrations make up a credible and practical reservoir of material, which I believe is free from the stiffness and sentimentality that often characterizes similar collections. Use them wisely and well as candles to bring light and cheer into the dark corners!

Illustrations

ADVERSITY

[1] Nature reveals that life can be transformed by taking something unattractive and converting it into something of beauty. By its chemical magic a tree or plant can take the dark soil and the waste carbon dioxide in the atmosphere and combine them with the aid of the healing warmth of the sun to produce green leaves, colored flowers, red roses, yellow tulips, blue larkspur, or a million other designs. By means of chemical processes we can take black coal and convert it into red dyes or synthetic rubber or nylon cloth. Faith gives life a similar transforming power—the power to take trouble or adversity and make it into something lovely and inspiring.

[2] People with inner strength and conviction seem able to find a way to overcome adverse situations. Jonathan Edwards was a strict Calvinist and a powerful preacher who helped mold the religious climate of 18th-century America. Yet, after a long-running dispute with his church council over standards for church membership, he was dismissed from the Northampton, Massachusetts, church that he served. He went to a tiny church in Stockbridge, where his major duty was to convert Indians. Most people would be chagrined, sick at heart, and discouraged to be treated so ungratefully by a Christian congregation, but Edwards refused to let adversity defeat him. He turned to writing, and his treatises had a wider and more powerful effect than his sermons.

[3] In hot tropical rain forests, huge plants and trees grow quickly, sometimes almost overnight. But these trees have soft wood, and they fall prey to insects and diseases and live only a short time. In the rugged mountains of the north, growth is slow. Plants and trees must endure high winds, ice storms, and intense cold, but they grow strong and tough with knotty, hard wood. Hardships have values we don't usually appreciate at the time, but they have a tendency to strengthen us.

[4] To go through life never conscious of any need, with everything like food, clothing, furnishings, and luxuries supplied to you, would be tragic. A wealthy man walking down a city street with a friend looked into a shop window displaying expensive jewels and remarked, "I'd give a good deal if I could find something that I couldn't buy." With prices as they are today, you may say the exact opposite: "I'd give a good deal to find something I *can* afford to buy!" But the lesson seems clear. If everything we wanted or needed were supplied as if by magic, without any effort on our part, life would become stale and pointless. There'd be no incentive for growth and progress. A sense of need and deprivation may at times be painful, but it has inspired humanity's best creative efforts and made possible our greatest discoveries.

[5] If I live long enough, I'd like to write a book on trials, because without them a person can neither know Scripture or faith, nor can he fear and love God. If he has never suffered, he cannot understand what hope is.
MARTIN LUTHER

[6] Early in the 16th century, William Tyndale completed a translation of the Bible into English and attempted to have it published. He could not borrow enough money for the job or even enough to buy paper, because such publications were illegal and Tyndale himself was regarded as a heretic. Finally he managed to issue a small edition of his Bible translation. Learning of this, the papal authorities sent their agents to buy up the copies of Tyndale's Bible at any price and to burn them. Sales to the papal agents provided Tyndale

with money enough to buy more paper and print a much larger edition.

[7] A hunting accident in 1858 blinded a young Englishman, leaving him depressed and despondent. Letters from friends did not help much, for they mostly urged him to be resigned to the will of providence. But one letter was different. It came from a former tutor of the 25-year-old man and said in part, "It will be your own fault if this trouble does not bring with it some alleviation. The evil that has fallen on you will lose half its terrors if regarded steadfastly in the face with determination to subdue it as far as may be possible." The letter went on with practical suggestions for study and plans for the future. It was the right challenge. Called on to accept his misfortune and make the best of it, Henry Fawcett became a professor at Cambridge University and later England's postmaster general.

[8] The greatest achievements of Hebrew religious genius did not occur during the peaceful, prosperous days of Solomon's glory. They took place when Israel was held in captivity in Egypt, through leaders like Moses and Aaron and Joshua, or in the disaster and slavery of Babylon. When things were at their worst, faith came to life, prophets came to the fore, and spiritual realities were asserted.

Christian history tells the same story. Its high points came not during the reign of medieval popes with their political power nor in times of prosperity and expansion. The greatest eras of Christendom were in the days of the apostles, persecuted, suffering, and scattered; in the days of the Reformation, when embattled believers struggled against entrenched power; and in the days of revival, when figures like Wesley and Whitefield demanded from their followers personal consecration and pious living. "When it is darkest, we can see the stars!"

[9] When beginners fall off the horse they are trying to ride, they are at once reseated on the horse. Too much sympathy or too long a delay can cause them to lose their nerve completely. The only place to get up is right where you fall down! It isn't easy, but it makes sense. The place where we fail is the place where we have

to win a victory, or we have failed forever. Jesus knew this when he directed the disciples to begin their ministry at Jerusalem—the place where they had seen him crucified, the place of Peter's denial, Judas' betrayal, Thomas's doubt, and the place where they had all forsaken him and fled. If they could develop the courage to witness at Jerusalem, they could venture anywhere.

[10] In the book *Who Walk Alone,* Perry Burgess tells the story of Ned Langford, a young American who returned from war service and established a good business in his hometown. His future seemed secure until it was found that he had leprosy. His first impulse was to commit suicide, but he resisted it. Placed in a leper colony on an island near the Philippines, Langford felt that his life had ended, conquered by an evil that he could not control. Then one day he saw a ruined building with lovely colorful flowers growing around it, making it a beauty spot. The thought came to him, if there can be beauty in a ruined building, why not in a ruined life? He began to look around for ways to improve his life and that of the other leprosy victims on the island. Using his business knowledge, he led them in organizing a fishing industry, and in a few years the island was transformed, with a new spirit and new values. Ned Langford, the leper, did more good than Ned Langford, the businessman, could have done in his hometown.

[11] The Bible never promises us a rose garden. It only says that God will not allow us to be afflicted beyond our ability to bear the affliction. God never shields us from the need to struggle and think and pray, nor even from suffering. He does not take life out of our hands, and we wouldn't want him to do so. We don't want to be spiritual weaklings, with God like a nurse feeding us with a spoon. As exercise develops muscles, so spiritual struggles develop spiritual strength.

[12] When a tiny toddler learns to walk, every step is an adventure. Stumbles and tumbles are frequent. A wise parent lets the youngster go on his dangerous expedition across the room, but is always ready with a helping hand to prevent disaster. God is like that, too.

AGE

[13] Count your garden by the flowers,
Never by the leaves that fall;
  Count your days by golden hours,
Don't remember clouds at all!
  Count your nights by stars, not shadows,
Count your life with smiles, not tears;
  And with joy on every birthday,
Count your age by friends, not years.

[14] Winter is on my head, but eternal spring is in my heart. For half a century I have been writing my thoughts in prose, verse, history, philosophy, drama, romance, tradition, satire, ode, and song—I have tried all. But I have not yet said the thousandth part of what is in me.
VICTOR HUGO

ANXIETY

[15] Worried about what may happen when "the bottom drops out"? That's a worry in Wall Street, because it could wipe out great fortunes. A dozen prophets of doom have written bestselling books to tell us how to confront the catastrophe they predict! It was evidently a worry in the days of Moses, too, but he found an answer. "The eternal God is your dwelling place, and underneath are the everlasting arms" (Deut. 33:27). When the "bottom drops out," God's everlasting arm is there to catch and support us.

[16] A Navy chaplain drew up a "Worry Table" based on the problems brought to him by the men and women he served. Their worries fit into five categories: worries about things that never happened, 40%; worries about decisions already made and not changeable, 30%; worries about sickness that never came, 12%; worries about children and friends, forgetting that they were able to help themselves, 10%; worries about real problems, 8%. His conclusion was that 92% of our worries are needless.

[17] Despite what some psychologists may say, fear has positive values in our lives. A small child without fear would soon be crippled or killed. Adults who plunge rashly into danger rarely come to a happy ending. We may admire the daredevils who perform on the television or movie screen, but for most of us a comfortable sense of fear keeps us safe. But fear is not only physical. Mental or spiritual fear can be more harmful than physical fear. We do conventional things because we fear being labeled a radical. We are polite to people who don't deserve it because we fear being social outcasts. We hoard things because we fear hunger or poverty. We get into a rut for fear of trying something new. When such fears dominate our lives, we need to conquer them in order boldly to stand up for what is right and true and progressive.

[18] Our anxieties sometimes occur because our will and God's will are speaking with different voices. God says, "Do this," and we respond, "No, I'd rather do that." It leads to civil war within ourselves. When we can sublimate our own desires and put our lives under God's command, as Jesus did on that dark night in the Garden of Gethsemane, we can say, "Not my way, but yours; not my will, but yours." The result is an end to the conflict of wills. It brings release, liberation, peace, security.

[19] It is not work that kills people, it is worry. Work is healthy and you can hardly put more upon a man than he can bear. Worry is the rust upon the blade.

HENRY WARD BEECHER

[20] Worry dissipates energy. Worry weakens you and saps your confidence. Worry makes you brood about questions that should long ago have been settled and forgotten. It keeps you thinking about life when you should be thinking about living.

[21] People do not avail themselves of the richness of God's grace. They love to nurse their cares and seem as uneasy with them as a man wearing a wig. Urged to cast their cares upon God, they soon take them up again. They take God's ticket to heaven and then put

their baggage on their shoulders and tramp, tramp, tramp the whole way there afoot.
HENRY WARD BEECHER

[22] Children are continually on the go, showing boundless energy and resisting any call to rest or sleep. They can wear out even a husky adult. When Mel Ott was the center fielder for the New York Giants, an experiment was conducted at a playground in which Ott tried to do everything a young child did. The trained athlete was tired out long before the child slowed down! How do children get such energy? Can it be because they are free from cares? They just romp about and let their parents do the worrying. Maybe even in adult life, we ought to enjoy our days and leave our worries to our heavenly Father.

[23] When I don't have anything to worry about, I begin to worry about that.
WALT KELLY

ART

[24] When Leonardo da Vinci was painting the famed *Last Supper*, he was said to have trouble painting the face of Christ. During that time, he also had a serious argument with an old friend and painted the friend's face on Judas. Conscience troubled him, however, and he repainted Judas and then turned again to the face of Christ, depicting it in the way that centuries have hailed for its beauty and spiritual insight. When we forgive others, our own problems may also be solved.

[25] On modern art: "So-called art today garlands the neck of the Muses with strings of garbage."
ALFRED NOYES

[26] My father was once given an antique rosewood desk, but somebody had slapped a can of cheap white paint over it. There was cherished beauty underneath, but to someone this value was meaningless. It took many hours of careful work to remove the white

paint and restore the old desk to its polished beauty. The person who had desecrated it simply lacked appreciation for its craftmanship and appreciation for its worth. People like that live in poverty, because they cannot see the real values in life.

[27] Tradition says that when Leonardo da Vinci was painting the great fresco of the *Last Supper* on the wall of the Dominican monastery in Milan, he decorated one corner of the huge painting with a charming little ship. People who came to see the painting noticed and admired the little ship, but after they left Leonardo took his brush and painted it out. He wanted nothing to detract from the central figures in the painting.

[28] Some people come to the Bible or to any work of great literature without the capacity to understand what is in it. They are like a person who comes to a well for a drink of water, only to find that there is no bucket to draw the water out of the well. When people say, "I didn't get anything out of the Bible" or out of the lesson or out of the sermon, it is quite possible that they came without the necessary equipment.

A man once walked through a great art gallery, looking scornfully at the paintings on the wall. "Are these the masterpieces?" he asked. "I don't think much of them."

The attendant standing by responded, "These pictures are not on trial. Their worth has been proved long ago. It is you who are on trial."

[29] When an artist wants to see his painting in true perspective, he often holds up a mirror and examines the picture in reflection. It gives him a different point of view, since the right appears left and vice versa. Another trick in painting is to place the work in a totally different light, to determine whether the colors still seem true and strong. Many artists simply turn a picture to the wall for a period of weeks or months, after which they can look at it with a fresh perspective. All these methods can be helpfully applied to life. When we face problems or decisions, a different perspective, a different light, a different time can all help .

[30] When Michelangelo was painting the *Last Judgment* for the Sistine Chapel in Rome, he was plagued by a pietistic cardinal who objected that nude figures should not appear in a chapel painting. Michelangelo considered the cardinal such an ass that he painted him as one of the lost souls in hell, complete with donkey's ears!

[31] The great statue of Venus de Milo stands in the Louvre in Paris. It has for centuries been regarded as an example of the matchless perfection of grace, dignity, and beauty. But when the German poet Heinrich Heine viewed the statue, he cried, "What was it worth? For she had no arms, the goddess, no hands to reach out and help poor beaten souls like me."

ATTITUDE

[32] When an English labor leader was elected to Parliament, he proudly took his daughter to see the great buildings where he would help make England's laws. The little girl was silent until he asked her, "What do you think?"

She said, "Daddy, you look so big in the kitchen at home, but you look small in this great big room."

[33] What's in a name? What does your name mean? Sometimes a name describes a person's occupation—Smith, Tailor, Gardener— or gives us information about the person—Redhead, Black, Short. Some names, especially in ancient times, were mere designations. Adam means "the man." Abraham means "father of many." Eve means "the mother." Isaac means "laughter," because Isaac's old mother Sarah laughed when she heard she was pregnant at the age of 90 and laughed again when she actually bore a son! In any event, a name distinguishes us from other people and gives us status. For generations, one of the most prized possessions a parent has been able to hand down to children is a good name.

[34] There's an old story about a princess who was unhappy because she was not pretty. A kind old aunt taught her three lessons: (1) smile at everyone she met, (2) look for all the beautiful things she could find, and (3) say something kind to everyone. The prin-

cess took the lessons to heart and soon was so popular and so busy that she forgot all about her looks. Instead, she gained a reputation throughout the land as a great beauty. A change in attitude reshaped her whole life.

[35] Contrasting attitudes toward life can be seen in statements from two men who are generally considered highly successful. Lord Byron, the poet, wrote at age 36: "My days are in the yellow leaf; the flowers and fruits of love are gone. The worm, the canker and the grief are mine alone." On the other hand, Adoniram Judson, a Baptist missionary to Burma in the early 19th century, wrote after a life of trials and hardship, "I suppose they think I'm an old man and it's easy for me to give up a life so full of trials, but I'm not an old man in that sense, and you know it. No man ever left the world with more inviting prospects, brighter hopes, or warmer feelings."

[36] Martin Luther found joy in his family during the later years of his life. One day his son Hans came home from school skipping and singing. "Why are you so happy?" Luther asked him.

"Today we finished the catechism," answered Hans.

"My, but you are far ahead of me," said Luther. "I've been studying the catechism all my life, and I haven't finished it yet."

[37] Our dislikes and prejudices are rarely reasoned out. They affect us in spite of ourselves. Tom Brown, a student at Oxford, expressed this well in this verse:

I do not love thee, Doctor Fell,
The reason why I cannot tell;
But this alone I know full well,
I do not love thee, Doctor Fell.

[38] It's not good to tell everything you know. Sometimes silence shows good common sense. Aesop tells in a fable about the lion who called a sheep over to him and asked, "Is my breath sweet?"

The sheep said "No," so the lion bit off the sheep's head for slander.

Then the lion called over the wolf and asked again, "Is my breath sweet?"

Seeing what had happened to the sheep, the wolf said "Yes," so the lion bit off the wolf's head for flattery.

Then the lion called the fox and asked, "Is my breath sweet?"

The fox sneezed and coughed and finally said, "I have such a bad cold that I really cannot tell."

The lion said, "Come with me. You are the wise one."

[39] Some people never learn to accept life gracefully. Like a dog with a bad temper, they're always growling, and we never know when they'll turn and snap. Their suspicion and hostility poison their relations with others and lead to cynicism. They are like Edwin Arlington Robinson's peculiar character, Miniver Cheevy: "Miniver Cheevy, child of scorn, . . . wept that he was ever born." On the other hand, some who suffer hardship and poverty still delight in the beauty of flowers or the freedom of birds flying high in the sky. They have learned the secret of making friends with life.

BIBLE

[40] In your home you have a small object that is more precious than gold, more powerful than dynamite, and filled with more blessing than a million good luck charms or medals. It's your Bible. It has changed lives, altered the destiny of nations, guided people in all ages, given healing to those in pain and strength to those who felt weak. Its pages of power give us God's assurance that he will fulfill his promises if we trust in him and that our highest hopes can be realized.

[41] The Bible is sometimes compared to a lamp to light our way. It reminds me of an heirloom, a lovely old oil lamp. The owners told me that they had found it tucked away in an attic, shoved aside with useless things that were to be thrown away. They cleaned the old lamp, had it rewired for electricity, and placed it in a prominent spot in their living room, where visitors always exclaim over it. It is a very old lamp, but it gives very up-to-date light. Similarly, some people think of the Bible as an old-fashioned light

like a smelly, flickering kerosene lantern, suitable only to be hidden in the attic, too dim for this age of neon lights and laser beams. Nothing could be farther from the truth. Like the light from the sun, moon, and stars, the light from the Bible is ageless.

[42] Once in a sermon I told an old joke about the biblical ignorance of our day. It starts with someone asking, "What are the Epistles?" Then someone else answers, "Oh, the Epistles are the wives of the apostles." The joke drew its usual appreciative chuckle from the congregation. But after the service, a woman as she was leaving the church said to me, "Pastor, I didn't get that joke of yours. If they weren't the wives of the apostles, whose wives were they?"

[43] There's an old story about a man who wanted to learn to read and write. Finally a visiting missionary offered to teach him, using the Bible as a textbook. The man learned rapidly and joyfully spelled out the words. The missionary had to continue on his journey, but some time later he returned to the community and looked up his former student. "How's the reading going?" he asked. "Still on the gospel of John?"

"Ah, no," was the reply. "I'm out of that long ago. Now I read the sports pages of the newspaper."

Isn't that typical of our generation? We got out of the Bible long ago and into everything else.

[44] When engineers charted the geography of the Shawangunk Mountains in New York, they came to a still, small, hilltop pond now known as Lake Mohonk. It seemed easy to measure its depth, but they tried several times without success. They returned with longer lines, but again fruitlessly. What they had assumed to be a shallow pond was really a crevice in the rocks, so deep that it seemed bottomless. Sometimes we share their feeling when we get into the great documents of our faith. We can read them over and over again, always plumbing deeper and always finding new depths.

[45] When Sir Walter Scott was near death, he asked one of his servants to read to him.

"What shall I read?" the man asked.

"Need you ask?" Scott responded. "There is only one book." His library was stacked from floor to ceiling with thousands of volumes, yet he thought of only one book—the Bible. Scott added, speaking to the servant, "Be a good man, be strong in faith. Nothing else will give you comfort when you lie here."

[46] A Sunday school teacher was dramatically telling the story of Abraham and Isaac and making it exciting. As she described the wood being stacked on the altar and Isaac being placed atop the pyre, one little girl nervously began to cry. "I don't want to hear any more," she said.

But the girl next to her nudged her and said, "Don't get worried. This is one of God's stories, and God's stories always come out all right."

[47] An old lady at her fruit stand on a city street was reading a book as she waited for customers. One man came along and asked, "What book are you reading?"

"The Word of God," she answered.

"The Word of God? Who told you that?"

"God told me himself," the woman answered.

"How did he do that?" the man persisted.

Confused, she changed the subject. "Mister, can you prove to me that there is a sun shining?" she asked.

"Prove it?" he exclaimed. "It proves itself. It warms me, and I see its light."

The woman smiled. "Just so, you are right. God tells me this book is his Word. I read it; it warms me and gives me light."

[48] If man could live by power alone, the hydrogen bomb would save the world. If we could live by bread alone, the productive wheat fields of the Western Hemisphere would be our salvation. If money were all, the mounds of gold stacked at Fort Knox in the Kentucky hills would be sufficient. But humanity does not live by power, bread, or gold alone. Our resources for living must meet spiritual needs—light in darkness, hope in despair, direction in

times of confusion, faith in days of doubt. Such needs are met by the Bible.

[49] Some people use proof texts lifted out of the Bible to justify their ways of life or their doctrines. If you lift such statements far enough out of the Bible, you can prove anything under the sun. You can send every enemy to hell, but you can't lead even your best friend to heaven because of the ugliness of such an approach. The Bible must be read and understood as a whole. When that is done, it shows us the gracious Christ, the loving God, and the comforting Spirit.

[50] People will defend to the death the Constitution of the United States. It is the bulwark of our liberty, the foundation of our nation. But, unless they were forced to do so by school assignments, how many of these valiant defenders of the Constitution have ever taken the trouble to read it carefully? Unfortunately, many Christians take a similar attitude toward the Bible. They'll quarrel over the interpretation of some narrow issue because they have never discovered the true spirit of love that the Bible declares.

[51] There's plenty of humor in the Bible. One of the gems is Isaiah's description of an idol maker. He pictures the idol maker at work. First he selects a tree and cuts it down. He uses a part of it to start a fire to warm himself and a part of it to cook his food. Then, warmed and fed, he still has enough wood left over for something else. What shall he do with it? He decides to carve it into an image of a god. Then he bows down before it, saying, "Deliver me, for you are my god."

How many idol makers we have among us today!

[52] Archaeology has in recent years verified many facts in the Bible, but other proofs pop up in unexpected ways. During World War I the British General Edmund Allenby conducted an expedition through Palestine and made one very successful maneuver simply because a staff sergeant was a Bible reader. The sergeant discovered that in ancient times the Israelites had captured one town by a

certain roundabout approach. He reported this to the general, and the British army repeated the Israelite effort with great success!

[53] The Bible is a tool to be used, not an ornament to be admired. Often people put the Bible up on a pedestal, admire it from a distance, entomb it in fancy leather covers, and make it a sort of idol. The bride carries it at her wedding, then packs it away with the souvenirs. The politician swears on it as he takes office, but seldom swears by it afterwards. The Bible is honored most when it is put to work in our daily lives.

BOOKS

[54] More than 3000 years ago the preacher of Ecclesiastes wrote, "Of the making of books there is no end; and much study is a weariness of the flesh." In ancient times famous libraries existed at Alexandria and Pergamum, as well as in other cities. In the Middle Ages, the Vatican library catalogued nearly 3000 volumes. Since then inventions like the printing press and electronic typesetting have multiplied the number of books. In Old Testament times, few could read. Now only a few cannot. Job cried out, "Oh that my words were written! Oh that they were inscribed in a book!" (Job 19:23) That was 4000 years ago, and today Job would have no need to worry. A man as rich as he would have a secretary at his elbow to take down every word and to rush them into print. There's no end to the making of books.

[55] They do not die who leave their thought
Imprinted on some deathless page.
Themselves may pass; the spell they wrought
Endures on earth from age to age.
THOMAS CARLYLE

[56] Books on the best-seller list are usually fiction, full of sex and violence. The books that have most influenced the world, however, were not best-sellers in the commercial sense. Besides the Bible, books that have the most effect in our lives today include John Bunyan's *Pilgrim's Progress,* Thomas Paine's *The Age of Reason,*

Karl Marx's *Das Kapital,* and Adolf Hitler's *Mein Kampf.* These books were widely read only after they had an effect on the course of the world.

BROTHERHOOD

[57] On a street in Westwood, New Jersey, three small churches stood near one another. A sign outside one church said, "We preach Christ crucified."

The second church had on its sign, "The Church of the Risen Christ."

In what may have been a spirit of one-upmanship, the third church's sign read, "We preach Christ crucified, risen, and coming again."

Maybe this was simply a symptom of competition and free enterprise. Or maybe it was a reflection on the disunity among Christians in our time.

[58] General propositions with regard to the love of God do not take a man one step outside the circle of the self. It is possible to combine enthusiasm for the doctrine of the universal brotherhood with an inability to live in brotherly concord with anyone.
From Man's Disorder and God's Design, *document of the Amsterdam Assembly of the World Council of Churches*

[59] Thomas Carlyle wrote of a poor widow who needed help. She lived in squalor, but her neighbors felt it was no concern of theirs and refused to do anything for her. As a result, she got sick and died. But before she died she infested the whole neighborhood with typhus fever, and 17 of her neighbors died from it. "She proved her sisterhood," Caryle commented. "Her typhus fever killed them. They were her brothers even though they denied it."

[60] The Jewish Feast of Purim commemorates the deliverance of the Jews from a pogrom or massacre planned by the wicked Persian prime minister, Haman. The prime minister was reportedly jealous of the Jewish wife of King Ahasuerus, Queen Esther, and obtained a decree that would permit him to annihilate all Jews. The queen

was sympathetic toward her people, but afraid for her position. She tried not to identify herself with her people. Then the Jewish leader Mordecai sent her a message: "Think not that in the king's palace you will escape any more than all the other Jews. For if you keep silence at such a time as this, relief and deliverance will rise for the Jews from another quarter, but you and your father's house will perish. And who knows whether you have not come to the kingdom for such a time as this!" (Esther 4:13-14) Esther got the message and reported Haman's wickedness to the king, with the result that Haman swung from the very gallows he had prepared for Mordecai. If righteous people do not stand up for the truth, if they keep silent, they too will suffer. We're all in it together.

[61] In the great prayer that Jesus taught, the first word is "our." We do not pray, "*My* Father," but "*Our* Father," and that's important. When we say "our" we can never ask for things that hurt others or ask for more than our share. God is everyone else's father, too. People we don't like or are worried about, people far distant and people we don't even know—he's their Father, too! As we realize this, a family feeling embraces all humanity, because everyone shares in the claim to be a child of God.

[62] One of the chief problems faced by the British during their occupation of India during Queen Victoria's days were the fierce tribesmen of the Garo Hills. They were cruel, dangerous headhunters, and the British decided that for their own safety they should send a strong military force into the hills and wipe out these people, destroying their villages and making the area uninhabitable. When a group of missionaries learned of the plan, they pleaded with the authorities, "Let us try first to solve the problem." Their plea was heard, and courageous missionaries fanned out into the area. Today the hills are dotted with churches, schools, and hospitals—a safe place for anyone. The message of love and brotherhood accomplished peacefully what guns and bloodshed could never have assured.

[63] John Masefield has a poem called "The Everlasting Mercy" about a drunkard who realizes the hopelessness of his life. If his

kind of life were all there is, a pigsty would be better! But coming to himself and awakening to the needs of others, he overcomes his problem and says finally, "I knew that Christ had given me birth/ To brother all the souls on earth." When we are awakened to God, we are also awakened to the needs of others.

[64] A man who has a thousand friends
Has not one friend to spare;
But he who has one enemy
Will meet him everywhere.
RALPH WALDO EMERSON

[65] Nature is a great leveler. How high is a mountain? How deep is the sea? The highest mountain is Mount Everest in Asia. It is 29,028 feet high or about five miles above sea level. The deepest place in the ocean is Mariana Trench in the Pacific, said to be 36,198 feet below the surface of the sea or about seven miles. On this huge earth, there is only 12 miles difference between the highest and lowest spots. And every rainstorm or snowstorm eats away from the mountains and carries away matter that helps fill up the ocean. Similarly, every human tempest—war, social revolutions, discovery, and scientific advance—levels the differences between human beings.

[66] The village of White Pigeon in Michigan is named after an Indian. In 1830 when white settlers came to the area, some of the local Indians converted to Christianity, and one of their number became very devoted to the white people. When he learned of a plot by some hostile Indians to raid the little village and massacre the whites, he ran 60 miles to warn his Christian friends. His valor was great, but the dash was too much of a strain for his body. As he staggered into the settlement shouting a warning, he fell dead. Today there's a monument in the village to White Pigeon. The inscription says simply, "Greater love hath no man."

[67] A story from Jewish folklore tells of a rabbi who had 12 sons. One son awoke in the middle of the night and prayed in a loud voice. His praying woke up his father, who demanded to know what was going on.

Self-righteously, the young man said, "See, I am the only one of your sons to wake and pray. All the rest lie here sleeping."

The rabbi answered, "My son, you had better sleep too, rather than wake up to criticize your brothers."

[68] From ancient times to the present, to eat and drink together has been a sign of mutual trust and confidence. In the Orient the sharing of a meal is regarded as a pledge that those eating together will not harm one another. If he has broken bread with his hosts, a traveler can feel safe in a strange house. This old custom carries over even into the affairs of state today. When an American president recently went to China and when a Chinese leader came to Washington, there was a great ceremonial dinner. It wasn't because they were hungry. Mere hunger could have been satisfied simply by going to McDonald's or Burger King, or to their Chinese equivalents. The formal dinners continued the ancient custom in which the participants pledged friendship. To some degree, the Jewish passover dinner or *seder* and the Christian rite of Holy Communion are outgrowths of this old tradition.

CHANGE

[69] James Hilton's novel *Lost Horizon* fascinated us with its account of Shangri-La, where nothing had changed for hundreds of years. Yet how dreary and depressing it would be if that were true; a child remaining always a child, workers forever in the same job, living in the same house, wearing the same clothes. In actuality, nothing stays the same for more than a moment. Nature's cycles are always in change, through the seasons and through the years. Trees sprout as seedlings, growing steadily through the annual cycles of bud, blossom, full leaf, and then dormancy, until the old trees die and fall to make place for new. The famous architect Louis Kahn pointed out that sunlight itself is never constant; it changes in direction and intensity every minute of the day, every day of the year. Change is part of the natural order and helps make life interesting.

[70] Columbus reached the shores of the Western Hemisphere in

1492 and other explorers came shortly afterward, but no permanent settlements were established for a century—and what a century! During that interval between discovery and settlement, Galileo lived, Shakespeare wrote his plays and poems, Luther nailed his 95 Theses to the church door at Wittenburg, the Spanish Armada was wrecked, bells tolled for the massacre of St. Bartholomew's Day, and a great rupture split Christendom. Only after this cataclysmic period with its great changes in philosophy, religion, and politics did European settlers establish permanent residence on America's soil.

[71] Sometimes you see little country churches standing alone and desolate and you wonder who ever built them there. Perhaps once they stood in the center of a community, but the people moved away and only the church building was left as a memento of the past. In Friesburg, New Jersey, a brick church built in 1714 still stands amid some fields and still serves a congregation, but the community that once clustered around the church is gone and hardly a house remains. Now the nearest town is the thriving community of Bridgeton, three miles away, but a faithful congregation still gathers to worship at the isolated church.

[72] Sameness and change are always in conflict. When people get bored or are troubled, they look for a change that brings new scenes, new excitement, new surroundings. Unfortunately, the people themselves seldom change, so they bring all their old hang-ups into the new scene. Happiness is not always produced by change; maybe it is *never* produced by change! Nature gratifies us by its monotony, with the same flowers every spring, the same snows every winter, the same sunshine, and the same rain. Children always seek to repeat pleasant experiences. Bounce a child on your knee, and he'll plead, "Do it again!" Tell a fairy story, and the child doesn't complain that Aunt Kate told her the same story last year. As a matter of fact, children love repetition to the point where they'll chide the reader if he changes even one word in a favorite story. It's always "Do it again" or "Tell me the story over again," and the great sorrow of childhood is that its joyous experiences cannot always be repeated, but are eventually outgrown.

CHARACTER

[73] Holiness and wholeness fit together. To be holy really means to be wholesome and healthy in thought, word, and deed. It means to "get it all together," to have an integrated personality. Holiness in that sense is a great need today.

[74] Translating faith into everyday life and action breeds character. Our beliefs and our actions must support one another. Leonardo da Vinci dreamed of a machine that could fly and even drew detailed plans for an airplane, but limitations of time and tools made it impossible for him to put his dream to practical use. Pels Manny thought up a plan for a machine to harvest and thresh wheat and even described it in a book, but it was left for another generation to produce one that could operate. These men were geniuses who achieved fame in other fields, but for most of us it is necessary that we carry our ideas through to a successful conclusion all by ourselves.

[75] A homeward-bound commuter fell asleep and awoke with a start when his train pulled into a station. Hurriedly grabbing his briefcase and coat, he got off the train just as it began to chug off from the station. Then, looking around, he discovered that he had gotten off two stations too soon and was still ten miles from home. The moral: Don't get off until you get to the place where you want to go.

[76] Building character:
Our greatest glory is not in never failing, but in rising every time we fall.
CONFUCIUS

There are no hopeless situations. There are only people who have grown hopeless about them.
CLARE BOOTH LUCE

If the steak is too tough for you, get out. The Army is no place for weaklings.
Sign in an Army mess hall

[77] Before the great bridges were built, travelers had to cross the Mississippi River on ferryboats. One of them was particularly dirty and run down. It creaked and shuddered as it went, and the engine room was deep in dirt and grime, with bilge water slopping around. One day it ran much better, and a passenger decided to go down to the engine room to find out why. He saw the brass had been polished, new red paint covered the walls, the floor was dry. An elderly black man sat in the engineer's chair, puffing at a pipe.

"What a change!" the passenger marveled. "How come?"

"I've got a glory," the engineer replied simply.

[78] Philosophers have always struggled with the problem of evil. John Newton observed, "Many have puzzled themselves about the origin of evil. I observe that there is evil, and that there is a way to escape it, and with this I begin and end." The fact is that evil can build strength, faith, and character. Savonarola said, "If there be no enemy, no fight; if no fight, no victory; if no victory, no crown." By facing and overcoming evil, we gain strength of character and increase our determination to do good.

[79] Norman Rockwell, the great American artist noted for his magazine covers, said, "When I want a dog model, I can always get it from the pound. Dogs that have taken a beating from life have character."

[80] Much of Sir Edward Elgar's fame as a composer rests on his great oratorio, *The Dream of Gerontius*, first performed in 1900. At the end of the original score the composer wrote, "This is the best of me; for the rest I ate and drank and slept and loved and hated, like another; my life was as the vapor, and is not; but this I *saw* and *knew*. This, if anything of mine, is worth your memory." Such testimony is the kind of thing that makes people stop, look, and listen. When you can say of something, "This I saw and knew," it expresses profound conviction. Can you speak as positively as this about your religious faith? If not, why not? But if so, then the power of your faith can make a dent on this unbelieving world.

[81] Can one little flaw destroy character? When a person has many

good points, dare we criticize one weakness? But one flaw can be fatal! The Greek hero Achilles was said to have been dipped into the River Styx by his mother to make him invulnerable, but she held him by the heel and that little part of his body was his undoing—his "Achilles heel." A similar legend from the Germans tells of Siegfried, who was bathed in dragon's blood to insure him from harm. But a leaf fluttered down and touched a spot on his back. That single vulnerable spot caused his doom.

[82] People can live on one of three levels. On the lowest level, life is too much for them; it masters them—beats, empties, and subdues them. On the second level, they are always battling life and never deciding, sometimes up, sometimes down. Most of us fit into this slot. On the third level, there are great souls who have conquered life and made their peace with it, living serenely. Put into different words, these groups might be classed as people without God, people wavering between two opinions, and people plus God. The secret to mastering life is found in the injunction, "Seek first the kingdom of God." The psalmist wrote, "I have been young, and now am old; yet I have not seen the righteous forsaken or his children begging bread" (Ps. 37:25).

[83] A best-seller some years ago was Dr. Walter Erdman's *Source of Power in Famous Lives,* which provided biographical sketches of 50 men and women such as Columbus, William Penn, David Livingstone, Jenny Lind, Clara Barton, Frances Willard, Oliver Cromwell, and others. Their source of power? "In their lives, God was a reality," Erdman wrote. There are many less famous persons who impress us with their triumphant living. They are hopeful in times of disaster, calm in times of crisis, helpful when things go wrong. If you were to search for the source of their achievements, you would almost always find that they were plugged into the power that comes from above. "In their lives, God was a reality."

CHARITY

[84] Charity is most effective when it roots out the cause of the problem. In a country village there was a deep ditch alongside a

road. With the coming of increased traffic, cars often failed to negotiate a curve and landed in the ditch. Nearby farmers stopped their work and used their tractors to tow the cars back onto the road. This happened often enough to interfere with the farm work, and finally a town meeting was called to decide what to do. "There's only one sensible solution," one farmer declared. "We've just got to fill in that ditch." Similarly, charity isn't just giving pennies or dollars to the poor, but rather changing conditions in order to prevent poverty and distress.

[85] The Holy Supper is kept indeed
In whatso we share with another's need.
Not what we give, but what we share;
For the gift without the giver is bare.
Who gives himself with his alms feeds three—
Himself, his hungering neighbor, and me.
JAMES RUSSELL LOWELL

CHILDREN

[86] At the police station in New York's Coney Island one Fourth of July weekend, I saw a room set aside for dozens of squalling children. In the course of a day, more than 100 children were brought to this room because they had either lost their parents or been lost by their parents. Fortunately, there was almost always a happy ending, police told me, as parents and children were safely reunited. Other children are lost under more desperate circumstances—orphans of war, unwanted youngsters, neglected tots. Even in affluent homes there are children who may become lost because they will go through life on false standards of materialism without any ethical or religious foundation. Lost children are a big problem in today's world.

[87] Famed actress Helen Hayes testified before a U.S. Senate committee on a plan to admit refugee children to the United States. One senator asked, "Would you adopt a child you never saw?"

Miss Hayes replied, "I didn't see my own child until after it was born."

CHRISTIAN RELIGION

[88] I am not a Christian, any more than Pilate was. But I am ready to admit, after studying the world of human misery for 60 years, that I see no way out of the world's troubles but the way Jesus would have found, had he undertaken the work of a modern practical statesman.

GEORGE BERNARD SHAW

[89] How careless Jesus was about his words. He flung them out into the Galilean air, and many echoed into silence in the surrounding hills. There was no stenographer or recording machine to immortalize them. Only what took root in the hearts and minds of his hearers remained in their memory and is preserved for us. His followers did not develop a religion of words but rather followed a way of life. They never told him, "You've given us something to think about." They said, "You have shown us God."

[90] In his play *The Coming of Christ* John Masefield includes a brief dialog between Procula, the wife of Pontius Pilate, and Longinus, a Roman centurion. Learning of the crucifixion, Procula asks, "Do you think he is dead?"

The centurion responds, "No, Lady, I don't."

"Then where is he?" she persists.

"Let loose in the world, Lady, where neither Roman nor Jew can stop him."

[91] When Charles Haddon Spurgeon preached in Scotland, an old man came to him after the service and said, "I am glad to meet you. I am the father of Henry Drummond."

Spurgeon responded, "Then I already know you, for I know your son so well." Later Spurgeon recalled his words and applied them to our relationship to God. The love, goodness, and mercy that we find in Jesus Christ make us certain that we know God.

[92] Every Sunday is a reminder of the resurrection of Jesus Christ. The resurrection changed the calendar, and the whole world has been influenced by it ever since we started to number our years as

"Years of the Lord." Enemies of religion often attack the observance of Sunday as the "Lord's Day" in the hope of undermining Christian concepts. During the French Revolution, for instance, special observance of Sunday was forbidden, and a new calendar was proposed that would set every tenth day as a rest day. But the conspirator who advocated this idea was soon murdered by other revolutionaries, and the proposal was doomed.

[93] In his novel *Bread and Wine* Ignazio Silone tells of an innkeeper in a remote Italian village who became convinced that one of his guests at the inn was Jesus Christ, because the guest had been exceptionally kind and helpful to a friendless dying girl. The innkeeper looked up the rules the Italian government provided for running a restaurant or inn. To his surprise, he found that there were no directions on how to handle the arrival of Jesus!

[94] Visitors to Rome's Rospigliosi Palace can see the painting *Aurora* by Guido Reni. It shows the chariot of the sun breaking through the clouds and driving away the dark. It is a great masterpiece of horses and clouds, youths and maidens, darkness and light. Unfortunately it was painted on the ceiling, so viewers cannot look at it long without getting a crick in the neck. But underneath the painting there is a large table with a mirror top that reflects exactly the painting on the ceiling. So Jesus came as a mirror to show God's love and mercy. For centuries, people stared upward to see God, but they grew weary. In Jesus, they could see God revealed in their midst.

[95] It's hard to believe that the entire life of Jesus was spent in an area about the size of Long Island, New York—an area smaller than the city of Los Angeles. His years were spent working among fishermen or people who lived in out-of-the-way villages, far from centers of communication or influence. There were no newspapers or magazines to report his miracles, no radio or television to broadcast his messages, no recording machines to take down his words. Yet by the providence of God, the story of his life and work leaped the barriers of time and space to storm the conscience of the whole world.

CHRISTMAS

[96] Modern America really celebrates two Christmases, the sacred and the secular. To most people, Christmas is a holiday of good cheer and gift giving that celebrates the winter solstice, the time when the days begin to lengthen and the sun starts its northward journey. We are really not far removed from the Druids of ancient Europe! The other Christmas is the hallowed event marking the day when Jesus Christ came into the world. Often these two aspects of Christmas clash. Somebody commented on a Christmas decoration, saying, "Oh, that's too religious." Can a sacred event be "too religious"?

[97] When you want to give the very best:
The best thing to give your enemy—forgiveness.
The best thing to give an opponent—tolerance.
The best thing to give a friend—your heart.
The best thing to give your father—deference.
The best thing to give your mother—conduct that will make her
    proud of you.
The best thing to give yourself—respect.
The best thing to give all people—love.

[98] We keep Christmas truly only when we let the love of Christ into our hearts and lives so that we can share it with others. We write *Anno Domini* in our dates, but do we really make each year a year of the Lord?

[99] Though Christ a thousand times in Bethlehem be born,
If he's not born in thee, thy soul is all forlorn.
English carol

[100] On Christmas Day in 1809 in Danville, Kentucky, Dr. Ephraim MacDowell performed a daring surgical operation for the first time, removing a woman's diseased ovaries. Outside the house a crowd gathered, threatening to lynch the doctor if the woman died! But the operation was successful, and the doctor, at great personal danger and sacrifice, had given the woman the best gift of all—the gift of life.

[101] Christmas giving is often just an exchange of tokens. One family had a long-standing Christmas custom of solemnly exchanging gold coins. If one member of the family would give out five gold coins, he would get five in return. It probably gave them a lot of satisfaction, but each person ended up with exactly the same amount that he started with. The best kind of giving does not expect a return or a reward. The best kind of giving is done anonymously to someone who cannot reciprocate or perhaps even say thanks, but who needs or deserves the gift. That's what God did on the first Christmas. It's an example worth imitating.

[102] "He who gives beyond his means to family or friends, does as great a wrong as if he puts his hand in another's pocket and takes by stealth that which is not his own." That was Russell Conwell's indictment of extravagant Christmas giving.

[103] Those who think religion is fading from our lives need to be reminded that in 1620 Governor Bradford of Massachusetts forbade the observance of Christmas Day. The first Christmas cards, a custom begun about 1860 in London, spread like wildfire until the Christmas card deluge has become almost a nuisance. But those early cards were cartoons or summer scenes, with nothing "Christmasy" about them.

[104] Two things are needed to make a gift real: a cheerful giver and a thankful receiver. Otherwise it becomes a formality or an exchange.

[105] The Russians have a Christmas legend of the *baboushka,* the old woman who was invited by the Wise Men to journey with them to see the child that was born. The woman refused, but later had a change of heart. She tried to catch up with the Wise Men but failed. Now, says the legend, she spends all eternity searching at Christmas time for something or someone. It's a depressing sort of Christmas story, but it has its counterpart in the experience of thousands who had their chance to find God but failed to take it.

[106] The birth of Jesus in a manger is a dramatic example of the

equality of all people before God. Suppose Jesus had been born in a palace; the Wise Men might have gotten in, but the humble shepherds would have been turned away at the gates by armed guards. Yet at the manger, shepherds and kings could approach on equal footing. God's gift is for all people. His love sent down not a delegation, a commission, an unapproachable monarch, but a baby!

They were all looking for a king
To slay their foes and lift them high;
Thou cam'st, a little baby thing
That made a woman cry.

[107] The danger of Christmas is that we observe it with legends and stories and holly and tinsel that can cover over the Christ child and prevent the real story from being heard. The heart of Christmas is not in parties or in pretty gifts but in what God has done. Cards, gifts, and celebrations can help make the season joyful and festive, but they must never blind us to the real meaning of Christmas.

[108] Sometimes we make fun of "holiday Christians" who come to church at Christmas and Easter but are rarely seen during the rest of the year. Yet we all feel a heightened consciousness of the reality of our faith at certain times. There are high spots in life when we really feel the strength of God's presence and are drawn into unselfishness by the knowledge of his love. Such moments are fleeting. The rush and tumble of life makes them fade. Back at the office or at the workshop, the old fears and irritations again take hold. Then we can only trudge through the valley, hoping that once again we may make our way up to the height. Maybe that's why Christmas and Easter come every year.

CHURCHES

[109] For 2000 years the Christian church has persisted and even thrived amid constant rumors of impending doom. At a time of threat to the church, Theodore Beza, a 16th century Calvinist theologian, said to King Henry of Navarre, "Sire, it belongs in truth to

the church of God, in the name of which I speak, to receive blows and not to give them; but may it pleas Your Majesty to notice that it is an anvil which has worn out many hammers."

[110] Intense rivalry developed in some smaller Scottish cities between adherents of congregations of the Church of England (Episcopal) and the Church of Scotland (Presbyterian). It even spread to the children, who delighted in taunting one another about the liturgical rituals on the one hand and the Westminster Catechism with its emphasis on the "chief end of man" on the other. They'd chant from the Presbyterian side:

Pisky, Pisky, bend and boo,
Up and down all service through.

To this the Episcopal kids would respond:

Presby, Presby, dinna bend;
Sit ye down on man's chief end.

[111] Is the church alive or dead? G. K. Chesterton describes the church as "rushing through the ages as a winged thunderbolt of thought and enthusiasm, a thing without rival or resemblance, as new as it is old." But Walter Lippman talks of it as a congregation of "grimly spiritual persons devoted to the worship of sonorous generalities." Which one is right?

[112] Every congregation has at least four classes of members. There are those whose names appear on the membership roll but who seem indifferent to the message or mission of the church. Then there are those who hear the message but make no effort to understand it. A third group consists of those who hear and understand the message, but do nothing about it. The fourth and highest— and often smallest—group consists of those who hear, understand, and act.

[113] A band of French Huguenots settled in 1550 near St. Augustine, Florida. Influenced by the Lutheran Reformation, they had fled from France to seek freedom of conscience in the New World.

41

Two years later their little settlement was attacked and wiped out by a company of Spaniards. "We kill you not so much because you are French but because you are Lutherans," the Spanish captain said.

[114] There are literally hundreds of recognized religious denominations in the United States. For example, a recent *Yearbook of American Churches* listed 26 "national" Pentecostal assemblies and 25 "national" Baptist associations, plus many regional and local groups. All of the hundreds of sects are seekers after God, yet they search in many different directions, as though God were up some special street or hiding in a particular patch of woods. Our crazy-quilt religious scene reminds me of the man who allegedly said to his wife, "Mary, I believe everyone in this world is crazy except you and me, and sometimes I even have my doubts about you."

[115] Most disputes in congregations are not about important doctrines, like those that were the subjects of discussion at the great councils of the early centuries of the Christian era. Today members of congregations are more likely to split over questions about the color of the carpet, the placement of the candles on the altar, or who should sing the solos in the choir.

[116] My communion is torn by factionalism. Some say we are baptized *into* the name of the Father, others hold that it is *in* the name of the Father. I belong to one of these groups, and I feel very strongly about it. In fact, I'd die to uphold the opinion of our group—but for the life of me I can't remember which one it is.
DAVID LLOYD GEORGE

COMMITMENT

[117] There's all the difference in the world between a thermostat and a thermometer. A thermometer tells you whether it's cold or hot, but it does nothing about it. Some people are like thermometers. They say, "The church is cold, the town is unfriendly, the nation is pagan." But they don't do anything about it! Fortunately, other people are like thermostats. When a thermostat finds that a

room is cold, it operates quietly to start the machinery to bring the cold room to an acceptable temperature.

[118] Plato records that Socrates said, "I am persuaded of the truth of these things, and I consider how I shall present my soul whole and undefiled before the Judge in that day. Renouncing the honors at which the world aims, I desire only to know the truth and to live as well as I can, and when I die, to die as well as I can."

[119] A medical missionary spent 34 years in China, building up a medical center and hospital only to see it wiped out by bombing during the war. To go back and start all over again after a lifetime's work had been destroyed seemed too much to ask, but he did it. Later there was a new hospital and near it a flower-covered grave with the inscription, "The winds of hate and storms of war could not root out the seeds that love had planted. Verily, some things endure."

[120] Edward Bok, in his book *Twice 30,* tells of President Woodrow Wilson's inner struggle at the Paris Peace Conference in 1919. One of his aides warned him against one decision, saying, "This will be risky for your personal prestige."
    Wilson answered, "That's not the question. My personal or political future doesn't matter. I know I cannot do the impossible things the people of Europe think I can. I know there'll be a tumble, and I'll be the one who does the tumbling. It's the cause I'm after, not what becomes of me. The cause!"

[121] When Montaigne was urged to become mayor of Bordeaux in 1571, he consented reluctantly to do so with one reservation: "I'm willing to take the city's affairs on my hands, but not on my heart."

[122] No person can serve two masters, but sometimes the choice is difficult. Dr. George Washington Carver, the famed black botanist, was offered a high salary by private companies that wanted him to work for them, but he rejected them all because he wanted most of all to help his people, the poor farmers and sharecroppers. John Knox, the Scottish reformer, was offered a large bribe to drop some

of his activities, but he chose to carry on his struggle for Scotland's religious freedom even at great personal hardship. More recently a distinguished young minister built up a strong city congregation. Some political leaders offered him a high-paying job as municipal chaplain, with duties that would require only a few hours each month. It was hard to turn down such an offer, but the minister felt it would compromise his preaching and his independence, so he turned it down. "I cannot serve two masters," he told them.

[123] A young doctor decided to go to India although his friends tried to discourage him. "You will be helpless against the suffering in that huge nation," they said. "You'll just be swallowed up in the mass of humanity. What can you do about their epidemics, wars, famines, floods?"

But the young doctor had only one answer: "When it is dark about me, I do not curse the darkness. I just light my candle."
EDDIE CANTOR

[124] Did you ever wonder how many times you have signed your name? Every check you write, every application form you fill out, every letter you sign, means one more occasion to write your name. In old-time contracts, in days when signatures must have been more rare, people solemnly certified their signatures by pricking a finger and adding a drop of blood to the page. It meant that they would give their lives rather than break the agreement, therefore the agreement was "signed with blood." While we don't follow this practice today, our promises to God are in a special way "signed with blood," because life and death depend on them.

[125] When President James Garfield was a student at Hiram College, he was always second best in Latin class. One other boy beat him out each time. One night as Garfield was about to put out his dormitory light and go to bed, he chanced to look across the campus and spotted the room where his rival in Latin class lived. The light was still burning in that room. *That fellow studies longer and harder than I do,* Garfield thought. *That's why he gets better grades.* So Garfield turned his light on again and went back to studying,

keeping at his books every night as long as the other light burned and ten minutes longer. Soon Garfield was at the head of the class.

[126] Mohandas K. Gandhi of India opposed the conversion of Hindus to Christianity. The *mahatma* himself was a well-informed biblical scholar, but never became a Christian. Someone asked him, "Why do you oppose conversion to Christianity when you try to convert the whole world to your social and economic opinions?"

Gandhi answered, "In the realm of the political, social, and economic we can be sufficiently certain to convert, but in the realm of religion there cannot be sufficient certainty to convert anybody."

COMMUNICATIONS

[127] Watching prime-time TV is like being trapped in Sleaze City's tackiest honky tonk. One gets a warped and depressing view of what it means to be alive.
TOM SHALES, *Washington Post* critic

[128] When the *New York Times* sponsored an Antarctic Expedition in 1928, it kept in close touch through its own radio station in New York. The chief of the newspaper's radio room, Fred Meinholtz, had his own radio receiving station in his home on Long Island. When he was at home in the evening, he usually listened to the dispatches from Admiral Richard Byrd's explorers at the South Pole.

One evening as he listened to words coming across 12,000 miles of ice, sea, and earth, he heard a voice break in and say, "Meinholtz, Hilferty at the *Times* wants you to hang up your telephone receiver so he can call you on the telephone."

Astonished, Meinholtz ran downstairs and found that his little son had evidently dislogded the receiver so that those at the office could not get a call through to him. He jiggled the hook, called the operator and was put in touch with Dick Hilferty, a *Times* radio operator.

Hilferty explained that he knew Meinholtz was likely to be listening to the broadcast from the South Pole and had therefore requested that the message be sent. To complete a call from Times

45

Square in New York to a Long Island home some 18 miles away, the message had traveled more than 24,000 miles!

COMPASSION

[129] If we knew the secrets in the hearts of others, we would be compassionate and not rush to judgment. Nathaniel Hawthorne tells the story of a clergyman who eloquently pleads with his congregation to overcome their sins but who in his own room wrestles in agony with unforgiven and unconfessed sin that gives him no peace. A news item tells of a banker who took his own life. Outwardly he was enviably rich, possessing beautiful homes, position, and power. But his wife had died, his son was alienated from him, he had no close friends, nobody to love and care for him. Many people have similar troubles, hidden sometimes by a brave smile or frenetic activity. But underneath, unseen, they are wearing sackcloth and ashes.

[130] In old Israel a king named Jehoram tried to keep up the spirits of his people while their city was besieged and facing famine. One day the king heard an appalling horror story, that a woman had turned cannibal and eaten her child. In despair, the king tore his outer garments of purple and gold, and the people discovered that underneath his fancy royal clothes their king was wearing sackcloth, the sign of mourning and penitence!

[131] The more sensitive you are to beauty and joy, the more you will be affected by the suffering around you. A dog, whose ears are so sensitive that he can distinguish his master's footsteps a block away, may howl in agony at the sound of a violin or a bell. If you are deeply concerned about the disease, disaster, sorrow, and suffering of our society, be glad that God has given you a sensitive heart.

[132] Like many great artists, Leonardo da Vinci was extremely sensitive toward pain and suffering of any sort. One day on the streets of Florence he saw a vendor selling caged songbirds. Da Vinci could not rest until he went back and bought out the vendor's entire stock. Then he opened the cages and set them free.

46

[133] In men whom men condemn as ill
I find so much of goodness still,
In men whom men pronounce divine
I find so much of sin and blot,
I do not dare to draw a line
Between the two, where God has not.
JOAQUIN MILLER

CONSCIENCE

[134] When John Wanamaker was operating his store in Philadelphia many years ago, he received a letter that enclosed 25 cents. The letter said, "I stole something from your store, and my conscience bothered me. It was marked $1.00 but I'm returning 25 cents because that's all it's worth. So now we're even."

[135] A computer can come up with the right answers only if the right information has been fed into it. Similarly, conscience is a proper guide only when it is formed out of the right experiences. In some primitive South Sea Island tribes, a youth was not regarded as a full member of the tribe until he had killed an enemy and eaten of his flesh. The tribespeople saw nothing wrong with this practice until Christian missionaries taught them differently.

[136] Because we all share in the sins of humanity, the innocent suffer with the guilty. In the sleepwalking scene in *Macbeth,* a doctor watches while Lady Macbeth moves about in agitation, crying, "Here's the smell of blood still. All the perfumes of Arabia will not sweeten this little hand." The doctor, with deep suspicions that he cannot utter, says, "God! God forgive us all." We often must feel the same way about the evil, injustice, and suffering in the world. God forgive us all!

[137] Unforgiven sin can be a great cause of anxiety and trouble. Thomas Carlyle wrote about a man trying to escape from his own shadow. Every time he looks around it's there, dogging his footsteps, following after him like a big black monster. He twists and turns to get away from it, but finally, panting and spent, he admits,

"O God, I can't escape. I can't get away." Unforgiven sin is like that, always in the background somewhere, threatening every move we make. King Herod experienced this feeling after he had killed John the Baptist. Months later he heard about Jesus. Trembling and frightened, he cried out, "It must be John back again—the man I killed, back from the grave to haunt me!" Only in forgiveness is there real peace.

CONTENTMENT

[138] We spend half our time wishing for things we could have if we didn't spend half our time wishing for things.
ALEXANDER WOOLLCOTT

[139] A businessman suffered serious illness. During his months abed, his business went to pieces. He regained his health but felt very depressed because his savings were gone and he had little to show for all his years of hard work. But as he walked through a hotel lobby, someone called his name. Hobbling toward him was a man who had lot both legs in an accident. With a big, friendly smile, the man said, "What's the matter, Bill? You look as though you'd lost your last friend!"

The thought struck the businessman with overpowering force: what wouldn't Jim give for my legs? If he had the money, he'd give a billion dollars. He realized in that moment the need for a change in his attitude, and he later told a banquet audience, "I'm a millionaire. I have a sound body, normal mind, fine family, and lots of friends, plus a job that gives me a chance to contribute my share to the community. I'm wealthy!"

[140] An old man seemed always cheerful despite life's troubles. "How do you keep so cheerful and calm?" he was asked.

"Well, I'll tell you," he said. "I've just learned to cooperate with the inevitable."

[141] Come, O Lord, in mercy down into my soul and take possession and dwell there. Give me Thine own self, without which,

though Thou shouldst give me all that ever Thou hast made, yet could not my desires be satisfied.
AUGUSTINE

[142] We find men today who do not praise the goodness of God because they cannot see that they have received the same things as St. Peter or any other saint, or as this or that man living on earth. They act as they do because they look above and not beneath. If they looked beneath them, they would find many who do not have half of what they have and yet are content in God and sing his praise. A bird sings its song and is happy in the gifts it has and does not murmur because it has not the gift of speech. A dog frisks gaily about and is content, even though he is without the gift of reason. All animals live in contentment and serve God, loving and praising him. Only the evil, grudging eye of man is never satisfied, because of its ingratitude and pride.
MARTIN LUTHER

[143] That little bird has chosen its shelter. Above it are the stars and the deep heaven of worlds, yet he is rocking himself to sleep without caring for tomorrow's lodging, calmly clinging to his little twig and leaving God to think for him.
MARTIN LUTHER

[144] How do you feel when the alarm clock rings to wake you in the morning? Grumpy and obnoxious? To judge by television commercials, that's the way many people start the day, somewhat like a bad-tempered bear coming out of hibernation.

A bad start can spoil the day. Why not try something different? Martin Luther suggested that the way to start the day is to awaken with a prayer of thanks to God and for your own needs. Then get up out of bed and hum, whistle, or sing a hymn while you shave, shower, or dress. Then read a few verses from the Bible and "go with joy" to your work.

This little exercise can change your whole attitude toward life. The few minutes it takes can be regained a dozen times during the day. And if you need more time, just set your alarm clock five minutes earlier. Start the day with God, see his glory in the morning, and let him work a divine miracle in your attitude toward life. It can make things new, as fair as when the morning stars sang together and the world was young, as fair as the gentle dewy dawn of a day in June, even if the snow is flying through the gloom outside your window!

COURAGE

[145] A novel published some years ago told of a man who believed he had an incurable disease. Doctors had told him that no remedy was known for the illness and that his death might be a lingering one. Rather than face long months on a sickbed, the man determined to invite a quick death. Somehow he managed to enlist in the Spanish-American War, where he recklessly exposed himself to danger. He led his comrades in battle and accepted every hazardous task, becoming famous as a daring hero. Then, near the end of the war, he learned that his doctors had made a wrong diagnosis. There was no immediate threat to his life from the supposed illness. Now, for the first time, he wanted to live, and for the first time the battlefield terrified him. Almost sick with fear, he once again led his comrades in an attack—and for the first time, he showed true courage. When he felt he had nothing to lose, there was no real courage in his daring deeds. But when he had to conquer fear and go on despite it, he became a truly courageous person.

[146] When Clovis, a fifth-century king of the Franks, heard a missionary tell the story of the crucifixion, he was deeply stirred. "Oh, if I had only been there with my Franks!" he exclaimed. "We'd have charged up the slopes of Calvary and smashed those Romans and saved him."

[147] Physical courage is a widely admired trait. We praise athletes who compete despite obvious handicaps, like the one-armed baseball player Pete Gray, or Monty Stratton, who pitched effectively although he had an artificial leg.

It's said that a lame man came to join the Greek army but the other soldiers laughed at him and said, "How can you run with that lame leg?"

To which the lame man replied, "I came to fight, not to run."

[148] At the Evanston Assembly of the World Council of Churches in 1958, honor was paid to Berggrav of Norway, Niemöller of Germany, Ordass of Hungary, Lilje of Germany, Kagawa of Japan, Kiivit of Estonia—all Christian leaders who had suffered persecution and imprisonment for their faith. Addressing the assembly, Bishop J. Bromley Oxnam said, "In deep humility I must confess that my faith has cost me nothing. Nothing! I have never suffered for the faith. I have never been hungry. I have never been in prison. I have never had a stone thrown at me. I have not been persecuted. My faith cost me nothing. I was born in a free land and possess a freedom won for me by my fathers. I have inherited a faith for which others died. I have read of faggot and lash for the goodly company of martyrs, but for me it has been too much a matter of appropriating the benefits of Calvary rather than of sharing in Calvary. I bow in respectful homage before my colleagues in this presence who know the meaning of the prison cell, of fetters, of hunger."

CREATION

[149] The first words in the Bible are, "In the beginning God created the heavens and the earth." Very few people ever question the truth of this simple statement, yet they argue constantly about it. The arguments are about how God did it (science), when God did it (history), and why God did it (philosophy).

[150] Could the universe have originated by some cosmic accident? People in every recent generation have asked this question. Isaac Newton, the famed astronomer who lived in the 17th century, gave one answer to it.

Newton argued with a friend that there must be a ruling intelligence, a primal first cause, behind everything that exists. The friend, however, insisted that the world was merely the result of a chemical process.

Newton had an astronomical globe made, a marvelous production of craftsmanship and knowledge. When the friend came into the room, he saw the globe and exclaimed over it. "What a wonderful thing! Where did you find it? Who made it for you?" he demanded.

"Oh, I just came into the room yesterday, and here it was," Newton responded. "It happened by chance to convince me of your theory of creation."

[151] For creation to happen without God would require odds of about ten trillion to one, according to Dr. A. Cressy Morrison. It's that unlikely! Morrison, a scientist and mathematician, wrote that science has learned a great deal since Darwin's day, and it all points toward the existence of a Creator.

[152] Ever looked at the mechanism of a watch? Only careful design and good workmanship can make it tick. If you were to take it apart, the chances are that you'd never get it together again. Certainly you could not just take its thousand tiny parts and shake them together and somehow make a watch that runs. Nor could you take a font of type and shake it together and by chance come up with a Shakespearean sonnet. Such things just don't happen.

Now take a look at the intricate adjustment of our universe. Every star and planet moves along its path in perfect order, so accurately that we can predict their exact positions thousands of years in the future. Or on the other hand, take a magnifying glass and study the instinctive orderliness of a beehive or an anthill. It all proclaims a wonderfully wise Creator.

[153] I believe in the God who reveals himself in the orderly harmony of the universe. The basis of all scientific work is the conviction that the world is an ordered and comprehensive unity, not a thing of chance.
ALBERT EINSTEIN

[154] That there is something of a nonphysical nature which controls the action of the universe is quite in the air today. It is possible to postulate a fundamental unity or order in which all living things, as well as all nonliving things, are controlled by something which possesses consciousness.
SIR JAMES JEANS

CROSS

[155] I can bear much, suffering the most distasteful things sent by the gods with calm courage. But four things I hate like poison and serpents—the smoke of tobacco, lice, garlic, and the cross.
JOHANN WOLFGANG VON GOETHE

[156] In the Louvre there's a painting of the crucifixion by the Italian artist Francia that would merit only passing attention except for the unusual sign on the cross. The emphasis is not only on Christ, but on a kneeling figure at the foot of the cross who looks up to the sign placed above Christ's head: *Et maiora sustinuit ipse* ("And greater pains than yours has he endured"). In times of pain and trouble and torture, this 15th-century artist evidently felt that this would be a comforting message of the meaning of the cross.

[157] Today we are accustomed to seeing crosses made of silver and gold, sometimes studded with jewels. They're beautiful, but there was nothing beautiful about the original cross. The cross was a gallows, made of rough wood, rude and ugly. Crucifixion was a cruel and heartless form of execution, and the executioners who carried it out had to be callous and hardened persons, taking the blood, the imprecations, the suffering, and the smells as part of their day's work. The whole thing showed sordid humanity at its worst.

[158] A Western city witnessed a strange phenomenon in the sky on a New Year's Eve a few years ago. Suspended in the sky above the city was a great cross of shimmering silver, blocks long and quite wide, startling against the blackness of the night sky. People stood in the street to see it, asking, "What does it mean? Is it a sign?" Soon the mystery was explained, however. A moisture-laden cloud hanging over the city caught the reflection of two lighted streets in the business section and mirrored them from the sky. That explained the mystery, but it remained uncanny and thought provoking—the light of the cross hanging over the city and the world.

[159] The shadow of the cross fell even over the early years of the life of Jesus. One artist worked it into a painting of the child Jesus at work in his father's carpenter shop in Nazareth. As a child stood with his arms outstretched, the bright sun shining through the doorway behind him threw a cross-shaped shadow across his path.

[160] In the hills of northern New Jersey stands a small church with the design of a large stone cross worked into one wall. Considering it an eyesore, one member offered a large donation to have the cross removed and a window placed in the wall instead. Another member responded, "What you want is not possible. The architect designed this church to have the cross. The cross gives strength to the wall, and if you ever remove the cross, you will destroy the church."

DECISION

[161] When King Gustavus Adolphus of Sweden was leading the Protestant forces in the Thirty Years War, he confronted the Elector of Brandenburg, who had tried to avoid involvement in the great struggle.

"This I say to you plainly beforehand," the king wrote to the elector. "I will hear and know nothing of neutrality. His Highness must be friend or foe. When I come to his border he must declare himself hot or cold. The battle is between God and the devil. Will his Highness hold with God? Then let him stand on my side. Will he prefer to hold with the devil? Then he must fight against me. A third position will not be granted to him."

[162] During the Civil War a well-meaning person said to President Lincoln, "I pray that God is on our side."

Lincoln answered, "I am more concerned that we are on God's side."

[163] A parade blocked a man's way as he went to keep an appointment, so he took a flag and joined the parade. As he marched along, he became so absorbed in the marching that he forgot all about his appointment and missed it.

54

[164] Paul Scherer tells the story of a wise hermit who lived in the West Virginia mountains. Some young men tried to fool him. They caught a bird and brought it to him, holding it in their hands. "What is it?" they asked the hermit.

"It is a bird," the hermit answered.

"Is it alive or dead?" the young men asked.

"As you will, my sons," the hermit said. "As you will."

So God places in our hands the power to do what we will with life.

[165] It's not necessary to have an opinion about Alexander the Great or Julius Caesar or Marie Antoinette or Queen Victoria. They are all dead and gone. They have little if any effect on our lives. But somehow or other we have to choose sides when we talk about Jesus Christ. Even the disciples were challenged by Jesus, "Who do you say that I am?" Even today you have to come to some decision about him. About the Creator God, it's different. You can't really choose to be for or against God, because God rules life inevitably. But belief in Jesus Christ and in his rulership is by our choice alone.

[166] A judge phoned a minister to say, "I have a real problem with a boy who claims to be a member of your church. He faces a long stretch in a detention center." The minister recognized the boy's name as one who had once attended Sunday school but had dropped out and rejected repeated urging to come back.

When the minister went to the boy's parents to ask their support, he was told, "We won't force him to go. When he gets old enough, he'll decide for himself." So he got old enough—and decided—but the police caught him.

[167] A simple creed: "I know there is infinite difference between right and wrong and that Thou lovest those who do right. Help me to do right."
HORACE BUSHNELL

[168] In the church of my boyhood, William Holman Hunt's famous painting *The Light of the World* was reproduced in a large stained-glass window. The picture shows Christ with a lamp in one

hand, a crown of thorns on his head, knocking at a door. Significantly, the door has no latch or doorknob on the outside and can be opened only from within. One little girl studied the picture for a long time, then whispered, "Mommy, did he ever get in?"

[169] A man needs three conversions: first the heart, then the head, then the purse.
MARTIN LUTHER

[170] President Ronald Reagan learned the need for decision making early in his life. A kindly aunt had taken him to a cobbler to have a pair of shoes custom-made for him. The shoemaker asked, "Do you want a round toe or a square toe?" Young Ronald hemmed and hawed, so the cobbler said, "Come back in a day or two and tell me what you want."

A few days later the cobbler saw young Reagan on the street and asked what he had decided about the shoes. "I haven't made up my mind," Reagan answered.

"Very well," said the cobbler. "Your shoes will be ready tomorrow." When Reagan got the shoes, one had a round toe and the other a square toe.

Says Reagan, "Looking at those shoes every day taught me a lesson. If you don't make your own decisions, somebody else makes them for you."

EVERYDAY RELIGION

[171] An old English painting shows a king saying, "I rule for all"; a soldier saying, "I fight for all"; and a bishop saying, "I pray for all." The fourth figure in the painting is a farmer who is taking a coin out of his purse and saying, "I pay for all."

[172] "Mind your own business," people advise. But what is our business? In the early morning an old woman went down a city street, picking something up from the ground and hiding it in her apron. A policeman watched for a while and became suspicious. He demanded to know what she was doing, but she did not want to tell him. "It's my own business what I'm doing," she said.

The policeman became insistent and threatened to lock up the woman, so finally she timidly opened her apron. It was full of pieces of broken glass. "Kids play barefoot in the street on these hot days," she explained. "I was afraid they would cut their feet."

Was that her business? Blessed are those who know that the good of other people is their business!

[173] The American people spend more for chewing gum than for religion. The reason is that they use chewing gum every day.

[174] History often seems dry and meaningless until it becomes personal in some way. Visit Mount Vernon or Valley Forge, or walk over the battlefield at Gettysburg, and it begins to come to life. Stand at the Wailing Wall in Jerusalem, and you can almost feel the presence of generations of the faithful who stood there to offer their prayers. We remember most distinctly things in which we have taken part or that we can at least visualize. Similarly, religion needs to be experienced so that it can become real in our lives. You can learn the Bible by heart or listen to a thousand sermons, but only when it is lived out in your own experience does religion become vital and meaningful.

[175] To separate the sacred and the secular weakens religion. People talk about God's day, God's book, or God's house as if these were exclusively the bearers of the name of God. Industrial leaders a century ago (and maybe even today) observed a very pious Sunday, but on Monday they opened their sweatshops and engaged in other dubious business practices. We need to realize that every day is God's day, that God's Word is not confined to the pages of a book, and that God does not live in a special house but is universal.

[176] Cornelia Cannon's novel *Red Rust* tells of a blight that affected the crops of pioneer farmers on our western prairies. It ruined the wheat and left them to face winters of poverty and starvation. They said, "It is God's will."

Finally one man said, "No, it's our own stupidity." They called him a heretic and made him an outcast, but he worked with others day and night until they finally developed a grain that could withstand the blight. It was really God's will that they should do something and not just blindly accept evil.

[177] Every individual stands before God, and every task is dignified and honorable, Martin Luther said. To be a monk or nun, segregated from the world by monastery or convent walls, was not necessary in order to lead a holy life. Every honest working person —butcher, baker, farmer, teacher, magistrate—is also serving God!

[178] Too busy to laugh, too busy to play,
Too busy to loaf for even a day;
Too busy to smile or walk a mile,
Too busy to see that beautiful tree
Or gaze a while at the open sea;
Too much hurry, too much rush,
No time to listen to the song of a thrush.
Too busy to live, too busy to love,
Too busy ever to look above.
At last at the gate I can hear Peter say,
"You're too busy. Please go away.
If I let you in, you wouldn't stay. You're too busy!"

[179] Charles Darwin in his later years admitted that his mind was a "withered leaf to everything except science." He could not even listen to the *Messiah,* which had once thrilled him. So it is always when the pressures of life crowd out from our minds things of the spirit. A few minutes of quiet and prayer each day can revive and revitalize both religion and life.

[180] The Bible says that God "makes the floods to cease." In a sense, God's people working together are doing the same thing today. A report from Pakistan tells of the tragic and costly floods that have afflicted the land for many years. People planted crops of rice and wheat in the rich lowlands, but time and again floods swept over the fields and drowned the crops and carried off topsoil. The result was often famine and death. Now Christians working together under their world relief agencies have provided the money

and technical advice to enable the Pakistanis to build dikes, dams, and diversionary channels so that the floods will cease.

[181] The best monuments are not markers in a graveyard but the things we do for others. In a New Testament incident, the disciples growled and criticized when Mary anointed Jesus' feet, but Jesus silenced them by saying that Mary had done a good work and "wherever this gospel is preached in the whole world, what she has done will be told in memory of her" (Matt. 26:13). There's a rabbinic saying, "Oil spreads its fragrance from the chamber to the hall; so a good name reaches from one end of the world to another." And so a good deed sheds its light into a dark world, building the most lasting monument.

[182] True religion permeates the life of the believer. We serve God whether we are working in a bank, teaching in a school, or doing any other sort of useful work. Religion is not limited to one small compartment of life.

Remember the old story of the three stonemasons who were working side by side. In answer to questions, one said, "I'm cutting stone."

The second said, "I'm making an archway for a door."

But the third said, "I'm building a cathedral."

All three were on the same job, but one had a vision of service far beyond the others.

[183] If we are cheated, shall we cheat back? Is retaliation ever right? An Episcopal bishop had to drive a great deal at night, often on narrow country roads. He would dim his headlights when other cars approached. But if the other car kept the blinding glare of its high-beam lights on, the bishop would turn his high beam on also. He called this, "A mild form of Episcopal swearing." But then he began to ask himself, Was it right? Who was being hurt? Wasn't he lowering his standards, even if he wasn't lowering his lights? If others were inconsiderate, was that reason for him to be unkind? He determined thereafter to stick to his own standards of conduct and never again to lower them, no matter what others might do.

[184] One of the most famous stories of all time is that of the good Samaritan, told by Jesus as an example of religion applied to life. The story is so vivid that many people feel that it must actually have happened. The same sort of thing does happen, over and over. It depicts three kinds of people.

First came the robbers, whose philosophy was, "What's yours is mine; I'll take it."

Then came the priest and Levite who passed by indifferently. Their attitude was, "What's mine is mine; I'll keep it."

Finally came the Samaritan, who ministered to the robbed and beaten man, in effect saying, "What's mine is ours; we'll share it."

And there is the fourth kind of person, the unfortunate victim of greed and indifference. The whole world is in this parable, and there's a little bit of all four types in each of us.

[185] A story by Tolstoi tells of a shoemaker named Martin who dreamed one night that Jesus appeared to him and said, "Look for me on the street tomorrow." With vivid recollections of the dream, Martin watched the street for the whole day, staring closely at everyone in the hope of seeing Jesus. He saw a poorly clad woman with a baby in her arms shivering in the cold. He brought the pair into his shop, fed them, and gave the woman a warm coat to wear. He saw a tired old street sweeper and invited him into the shop to sit down for a rest and have a cup of coffee. He saw an apple seller quarreling with a street urchin and taught them to make peace with one another. That was all. It was a dull, disappointing day, and Martin went to bed feeling defeated. But the dream occurred again, and Jesus said to him, "Martin, did you not know me? Inasmuch as you did it to the least of these my brethren, you did it to me."

EXAMPLE

[186] A few years ago many experts solemnly warned us that we must expect shortages in almost everything—oil, gasoline, steel, grapefruit, mortgage money, and paper! There seemed to be a looming shortage of everything except trouble. It made me think of our greatest shortage today—a shortage of heroes and heroines. Who can children look up to and emulate? To be sure, we have plenty

of "stars," athletes and entertainers, but very few great men or women.

[187] A Supreme Court justice went to a small Vermont village for his summer vacation. The village church was run-down and neglected, but to the surprise of the villagers on the first Sunday after his arrival, the judge drove into town and attended the church service. When he did it again the following week, the people began to wonder if they were missing something. Word got around about the judge's churchgoing, and many who had not been in the church for months decided to see what was going on. They quickly noted that the building needed repairs and painting. If the judge was planning to attend regularly and perhaps bring influential friends with him, they wanted to make a better showing. So the building was patched up, and the whole congregation rejoiced in the improvements. The spiritual tone of the whole community was lifted —all because of one person's loyalty to the church.

[188] A young student torn by doubt and indecision walked the streets of his college town all night in an effort to resolve his perplexities. Early in the morning he noticed that a church was open, with a service in progress. He went in and sat quietly in the shadows in a rear pew. As he looked over the little congregation, he saw one of his teachers bowed in reverence. "Surely if this excellent teacher has faith in God, there must be a satisfactory answer to my problems," he thought. The incident led him into new directions that helped him find the solutions he sought. The teacher may never have suspected that his presence in church on that morning would give strength and guidance to the student. Without saying a word, he had given eloquent and forceful testimony.

[189] Perhaps some people can still remember the days when city streets were lighted by gas lamps. At dusk a lamplighter walked down the street with a long pole with a lighter at one end. As he went, he stopped at each lamp post to turn on the gas and light the lamp. As he went along his way, the street was brightened. Even after he had turned a corner and passed from view, a trail of light remained behind him. We all ought to resolve to live in such a

fashion as to leave a trail of light behind us, to guide the steps of those who follow. Alexander Cruden suggested, "Let your gifts and graces be so apparent to others in your way of teaching and living that they may be brought to own and believe in the true God and to look upon you as his true and faithful servant."

EXCUSES

[190] According to a biblical parable, a rich man gave a banquet and invited guests, but they all made excuses. One said he had bought a plot of ground and needed to see it; another needed to try out a new yoke of oxen; a third had just married a wife! In our time those alibis for rejecting the gospel have a strangely familiar sound. What minister or evangelist has not heard, "I've bought a new house and Sunday is the only day I have to work on it." "I've bought a new car and Sunday I have to take it out on the road and test it." "My husband doesn't feel like coming, and I can't come alone."

[191] As a U.S. Army hospital ship was steaming into the combat zone in the Pacific during World War II, special chapel services were held for those of the Roman Catholic, Protestant, or Jewish faiths. Because of the imminent danger, there was a record turnout. One doctor attended all three services. When his colleagues kidded him about this, he said, "Listen! At a time like this I'm taking no chances."

FAITH AND DOUBT

[192] If I could not doubt, I should not believe.
HENRY THOREAU

[193] There lives more faith in honest doubt,
Believe me, than in half the creeds.
ALFRED TENNYSON

[194] I was never under greater nervous strain than during our in-vasion of North Africa. One night I rolled and tossed until my wife

62

asked me why I did not go to sleep. I said I just couldn't seem to relax, and she said she would read me to sleep. I asked her from what, and she said from the Bible, the one I carried in the other war.

She happened to open it at one of those fighting Psalms, where the old boy was praying to God to help him lick his enemies. I soon began to chuckle and pretty soon went to sleep.
FRANK KNOX, Secretary of the Navy during World War II

[195] There are honest doubters, but no honest atheists. Everybody has a god, but not everybody knows the true God. Martin Luther commented, "What does it mean to have a god? Whatever your heart clings to or relies upon, that is properly your god."

[196] I need not shout my faith. Thrice eloquent
Are quiet trees and the green listening sod.
Hushed are the stars, whose power is never spent;
The hills are mute—yet how they speak of God!
CHARLES HANSON TOWNE

[197] A well-educated woman once said to me, "It isn't that I don't believe in God. The problem is that I haven't the least idea what you mean by the word."

[198] Everything we do is directed by what we believe, what we put our faith in. You put money in a bank because you trust the bank and believe your money will be safe. You work at a job because you believe you are doing good, or at least you believe that you'll be paid. You take medicine because you believe that it will help you. All life is rooted in faith.

Robert Browning wrote, "Belief or unbelief bears upon life, determines its whole course, begins at its beginning." All we do is regulated by what we believe.

[199] King Croesus of Lydia was reported to be the richest man in the world. It was rumored that everything he touched turned to gold. More than he wanted gold, however, he wanted wisdom, so he summoned the philosopher Thales and asked him, "What is

God?" For the answer to this question, Croesus promised, he would pay whatever sum Thales wanted. The philosopher deliberated for days and weeks, but the more he searched the more elusive the answer seemed. Finally he had to admit that he could not answer the king's question. Many years later the Christian writer Tertullian said that the incident was an example of the world's ignorance without Christ. "The wisest man in the world could not tell who God is," he wrote. "Yet the most ignorant mechanic among Christians knows God and can proclaim him to others."

[200] In *Pilgrim's Progress* John Bunyan writes about a pilgrim locked in the castle of Giant Despair, in its very deepest dungeon. The pilgrim is about ready to give himself up for lost, when he recalls that in a pocket he carries a key called "Promise" which is able to unlock any dungeon door. Actually, we all have such a key. Faith is the key.

[201] I bless myself and am thankful that I never saw Christ or his disciples. I would not have been one of those Israelites that passed through the Red Sea, nor one of Christ's patients on whom he wrought his miracles, for then my faith would have been forced on me. I enjoy the greater blessing of those who saw not and yet believe.
SIR THOMAS BROWNE

[202] During the reconstruction period after a war, an international meeting was held in France to determine how ruined lands could best be restored. One delegate said, "We need the two *f*'s— food and fuel." Another delegate added a third *f*—fertilizer. Then a French representative said, "America has a fourth *f* more important than these three, and that's what we need most—faith."

[203] When people speak of "securities," they usually mean bonds, mortgages, bank books, or money. Most of us possess a dollar or two, but have you ever looked closely at a dollar bill? It's a scrap of paper, printed in green ink. What gives it value is the promise printed on it by the government. The value of that bill lies in its promise and in the faith we have in the government that makes

the promise. We believe that promise, and so we say the little piece of paper is worth one dollar.

[204] Faith, according to Charles Haddon Spurgeon, is knowledge, belief, and trust, but all three must be present. He described faith in Jesus Christ as meaning, "*F*orsaking *a*ll *I* *t*ake *h*im."

[205] Faith is to believe what we do not see, and the reward of faith is to see what we believe.
AUGUSTINE

[206] What we believe influences what we do. In a village in India a missionary found that his greatest struggle had to be against ideas and beliefs. When a cholera epidemic broke out, the villagers held to their belief that the cholera demon was the cause of the disease. They engaged in constant loud shouting and beating of drums to frighten away this demon, hindering the work of doctors and nurses and driving everyone to distraction. It was a painful example of the power of belief, however misguided it may be.

[207] Johann Wolfgang von Goethe, great German poet and dramatist, was an agnostic but not an atheist. He simply could not decide what to believe. As he grew older, the constant terror of insecurity and indecision affected him, and on his deathbed his final words were, "More light." Those attending him pulled up the shades to let more daylight into the room, but it didn't satisfy the old man. He repeated, "More light!" As the darkness of death gathered over him, the light he craved was spiritual. What the world needs even today is more light—not the kind of electrical wizardry that turns night into day, but the light of spiritual understanding.

[208] Two small boys were arguing about the existence of the devil. "There isn't any devil," said one of them. "It's like Santa Claus. It's your father."

[209] Among the detours and side issues of life, we need faith to keep us heading in the right direction. Faith is to life what a com-

pass is to those who steer a ship. If you have ever rowed a boat on an open lake or sea, you know that the natural tendency is to pull more heavily on one oar than on the other, with the result that you go around in circles. A similar experience can afflict people lost in the woods, who confidently try to find their way out only to circle around to the starting point. Without a compass or guidepost, you can get lost.

[210] Faith makes God's power and grace effective in our lives. Where there is no faith, God cannot get through. Perhaps a good example would be the radio waves that at this very moment are here, all around you and even inside of you. They permeate everything, but without a receiver that will catch these signals and permit you to hear them, they are unrecognized and useless. Remember that in one place during his ministry, Jesus could do no miracle because of their unbelief. If God is not as powerful in your life as he should be, look within. Maybe your receiver is turned off. Faith can make you filled with God's power; or, by its absence, it can make you helpless and miserable.

[211] Three testimonies to faith in God:
   Nothing can be greater than God, for God is subject to nothing and rules the universe.
CICERO

   God is of surpassing power and eternal, invisible to every mortal creature but yet seen in the works he does.
ARISTOTLE

   "Is the sun the maker of all things? He who makes must abide with what he has made; the sun is absent, so he cannot be the universal creator. The sun must have a lord and master greater than himself."
INCA YUPANQUI *in Peru, about* A.D. *1440*

[212] Jesus died. That's history.
Jesus died for me. That's faith.

66

FAITH AT WORK

[213] In *Les Miserables* Victor Hugo tells of a bishop who was assigned to a 60-room mansion. Across the street from the bishop's mansion was a six-room hospital. One day the bishop crossed the street and asked, "How many patients have you here?" He was told there were 26 patients. "In six rooms?" the bishop asked. "Yes," they said, "We are very crowded."

"Obviously there has been some mistake," said the bishop. "You shall have my house, and I will take yours. Move your patients."

So the sick people were moved into the 60-room mansion, and the bishop moved into the little one-story hospital, but the people in the town were amazed and disturbed. "He doesn't act like a bishop," they complained.

[214] A Christian's task is not to talk grandly of doctrine, but always to be doing hard and great things with God.
ULRICH ZWINGLI

[215] The Scottish entertainer Sir Harry Lauder always left his audiences laughing. But as he came out of a theater one night, he was handed a telegram informing him that his son had been killed in action. Lauder canceled his engagements, but three weeks later he was on his way to France to entertain the troops. "When a man has a great sorrow," Lauder said, "he can turn sour on life, or turn to drink, or turn to God and find joy and hope in doing his will."

[216] When persecution and evil began to spread through Germany, I looked first to the universities, the great free centers of learning, for opposition. They were soon wiped out. Then I looked to the press, the newspapers and magazines of wide circulation and great power. They were soon suppressed. It was only in the Christian churches and Christian pulpits that men dared to stand up for the right and truth and freedom.
ALBERT EINSTEIN

[217] "Everything that many of us have accepted, grown up with, perhaps taken for granted, is being thrown into the melting pot,"

said Bishop John Phillips of Portsmouth, England. He was expressing alarm at the rapid changes taking place in church and society, but those changes give us the chance for renewal or replacement of worn or outmoded parts.

[218] Wampus Pond near Mount Kisco in New York State was desolate, stagnant, and choked with weeds and debris when I first saw it. It was a place only frogs and watersnakes could love. But one day as I drove by, it was changed. Instead of weeds, there were lilies. The old tires and old junk had been removed and the water was clear. Newly planted pine trees lined the shore. It was the same pond and in the same place, but it had a new look. That's what renewal or newness of life means!

[219] Saints Cassian and Nicholas had an argument. Cassian said study, prayer, and devotion were the proper roles for a saint. When Cassian died and went to heaven, the Master asked, "What did you see on earth?" Cassian said he saw a peasant whose wagon was stuck in the mud.

"Did you help him?" the Master asked.

"No," said Cassian. "I did not want to soil my nice white robe."

Shortly afterward Nicholas arrived, flushed with exertion, muddy and dirty. "How did you get so dirty?" the Master demanded.

"I saw a peasant and his wagon stuck in the mud, so I put a shoulder to the wheel and helped him out," responded Nicholas.

"You did well, far better than Cassian," said the Master. "Your robe will be white for all eternity." When Nicholas looked down, he saw that his robe was gleaming spotless white, but Cassian's robe had become stained with mud and dirt.

[220] The only way to discover the power of faith is to put it to the test. On test runs new automobiles are driven for days without stopping. Tires wear out and are replaced, the oil is changed, but the grueling test goes on for many thousands of miles to see how the car performs and stands up under hard use and difficult conditions. Similar tests are given to airplanes. Engineers can chart their expected performance on the drafting board, but until the plane soars into the sky and is put through its paces, its qualities are not

fully known. So it is with faith; its latent power may be present in our lives, but we get its full benefits and assurance only when we use it and put it to the test.

FAITHFULNESS

[221] At the time of Jesus, Hebrew was already a dead language. The spoken tongue was Aramaic. Yet even today all over the world thousands of Jewish children learn Hebrew. It is used for official documents in the land of Israel. This tenacity of language is more than stubbornness. It is a sign of the determination of this ethnic group to keep its identity. Scattered, beaten, battered, cursed, consigned to inferior status for centuries, the Jews have nonetheless consistently clung to their faith. Whether or not those around agree with them, the Jewish people hold to their faith and pass it on to their children. It is an admirable trait.

[222] During the Franco-Prussian War, a young lieutenant was seriously wounded. As he lay dying on the field, attendants came to try to move him back from the danger zone, but he refused attention. "Let me die here where I can see the emperor," he insisted. So they left him and went on to attend to others. Later they came back and took up his body. Underneath it were his regimental colors! He had given his last chance for life rather than let them retreat or fall into the hands of the enemy. When they buried him on the battlefield they wrapped the flag around him, a tribute to his faithfulness even to the brink of death. That kind of loyalty is what God expects of us: "Be faithful even to death. . . ."

[223] In colonial times there was one day of unaccountable darkness. It seemed as if the sun had not risen, for blackness covered the sky and it seemed like night. People were alarmed and some feared it might mean the end of the world. When the Connecticut legislature convened at noon, some legislators expressed their fears and wanted to adjourn the session, but one Puritan said, "If the day of judgment has indeed come, I desire to be found at my post doing my duty." His point of view prevailed. Candles were brought into the room and lighted so the session could proceed with business

as usual. Really, we ought to live every day as though it were our last day; and if it is the last day, we should be found doing our work as honestly and well as we are able.

[224] The man who once most wisely said,
"Be sure you're right, then go ahead;"
Might well have added this, to wit:
"Make sure you're wrong before you quit."

FALSE HOPES

[225] During World War II, the "cargo cult" developed among the primitive and superstitious natives of New Guinea. As they watched the American soldiers, they observed that whenever something was needed, a merchant ship or plane brought it in. They decided that there was some magic about this, and connected it with the army uniforms. Eagerly they made off with discarded uniforms and even stole uniforms, expecting that this would give them the power to obtain valuable materials, presumably from the white men's gods. Maybe they are still waiting.

[226] Christopher Morley writes of a man relaxed in a barber's chair, his face lathered, enjoying the attention. Suddenly a boy comes to the door of the barber shop shouting, "Mr. Schultz! Mr. Schultz! Your house is on fire."

The customer jumps up from the chair, tears the apron off and runs down the street, lathered face and all. He goes a full block before he stops and says, "What the deuce am I doing? My name isn't Schultz!"

Morley says it reminds him of how often he's spent time and energy running to someone else's fires.

[227] At the World's Fair in 1939 at San Francisco, one of the attractions was a pile of money said to total $1,000,000. For 25 cents, visitors were allowed to touch the money. Were they any richer for it, or were they just 25 cents poorer? False ideas and false ideals can rob people even of the little they have!

FREEDOM

[228] There are two freedoms: the false, where a man is free to do as he likes, and the true, where a man is free to do as he ought.
CHARLES KINGSLEY

[229] A Christian is a perfectly free lord of all, subject to none, but also the dutiful servant of all.
MARTIN LUTHER

[230] The Christian life can do all things and has all things and lacks nothing. It is the lord over sin, death, and hell, and yet at the same time it serves, ministers to, and benefits all mankind.
MARTIN LUTHER

[231] A lawyer made an impassioned plea on behalf of a client who had been accused of murder. The jury was impressed and came back with a verdict of not guilty. Freed from the shadow of death row, the accused man hurried over to the lawyer to thank him, but the lawyer ignored his outstretched hand and turned away in disgust. "Get away," he said to his former client. "You're as guilty as hell itself." The man had won freedom, but not forgiveness—and there's a difference.

[232] It has always amused me that religious groups end their meetings with the Old Testament benediction, "May the Lord watch between me and thee when we are absent one from another." That statement arose out of Laban's distrust for his son-in-law Jacob and called upon God to witness that Jacob did not mistreat Laban's daughters or take other wives! But sometimes a little distrust can lead to strengthened policies that work for the good of all. The founding fathers of the American nation were wary about trusting each other completely. The Virginia Episcopalians feared that the New England Congregationalists might try to impose their way of worship upon the whole country, and vice versa. Out of this distrust came the firm decision that Congress make no law establishing a religion, the great First Amendment that has ever since been hailed as the cornerstone of our liberties.

[233] Nobody likes to be in prison, behind locked doors, but sometimes we shut ourselves up in a sort of prison and lose our freedom. Fear of what people will say, or fear of the future, locks us in a gloomy dungeon. Memory, particularly of some shameful or unhappy experience, can shut us up into the past. Resentment against others or against God himself can shut the door on life. Self-absorption is the most typical door closer. Bondage to our own desires or pleasures and indifference to others keeps us in a prison of our own making. We lose and the world loses until we allow the chains that bind us to be broken. When fear and guilt and resentment and selfishness are removed by our commitment to Christ and his love, life can be new and fresh and free.

[234] Most youngsters have at some time flown a kite. They had great fun taking it out to a breezy meadow and watching it soar up into the sky as far as the string would permit. One lad felt that his kite deserved complete freedom, so he let go of the string, expecting to see the kite rise higher and disappear from sight, but instead the kite began to swoop and dip. In a matter of minutes it had fallen to the ground. Without the restraint of the string, the kite came to grief. Absolute freedom will do that to kites and to people. A kite without a string, a ship without a rudder, an automobile without brakes, or a human life without the restraint of conscience and the commandments—they all add up to trouble. Without the necessary restraints, whether they are the laws of God or of nature, freedom leads to tragedy.

[235] One of the most precious words in our language is *freedom*, but true freedom is not merely liberty to do what we like. It is freedom to do what we ought, to be at our best, to obey conscience. Such limits are necessary lest freedom dissolve into waste and dissipation. Roses in the garden need to be pruned, which certainly is an infringement on their liberty to grow as they please. But without pruning, the strength of the plant would be drawn off into straggly shoots that would diminish the size and beauty of the roses. To be at their best they need to be restrained, either voluntarily or by a gardener's pruning shears. That's why we speak of "liberty under

law," for only by such restraint can we be at our best, free to love and serve one another.

[236] "The condition upon which God hath given liberty to man is eternal vigilance," said the Irish patriot John Philpot Curran. More modern phrasemakers are more likely to say, "There's no such thing as a free lunch." Freedom has a price; it must be earned, nurtured, and defended.

[237] We are free only to the degree that we use the privileges of freedom. Many times we are like a little dog who hated to be tied up. With nothing else to do, the dog gnawed at the leather leash that restrained him and finally chewed the leash in two. Yet he sat quite still because he did not realize that he was free! So the freedom that God gives us becomes ours only when we accept it and use it. A poet wrote:

> The sweet compulsion of His voice
> Respects the sanctity of will.
> He giveth day; thou hast the choice
> To walk in darkness still.

FUTURE

[238] A well-known businessman received a letter from someone who enclosed a stamped reply envelope with the request, "In the enclosed envelope kindly send me information about what business conditions will be like six months from now."

The man replied, "For the price of a stamp you want to know something that I would gladly give one million dollars to know right now."

[239] Mariners' charts in the 16th century outlined rather crudely the shoreline of Europe and Africa, but out in the Atlantic, where few had ever ventured, were statements like "Here be dragons" or "Here be demons that devour men." Being unknown, the area seemed dreadful and frightening. We always seem to fear the unknown. But every living person is proceeding constantly into unexplored territory. No one has ventured into tomorrow, but we'll

all be into it in 24 hours. Our light is not bright enough to see what it will bring, but our faith is sufficient to make us go unafraid.

[240] During World War II a conference on the future was held at Malvern in England. Among its findings was the conclusion that if civilization was "to survive after the war, it must become a cooperative commonwealth in which earth and its resources are treated no longer as a reservoir of potential riches to be exploited, but as a storehouse of divine bounty on which all utterly depend."

[241] Scientists generally believe that human life began either in Mesopotamia in Asia Minor or somewhere in Africa. It spread eastward into Asia and then gradually westward to Greece and Rome and finally western Europe. There it came to a dead end. There was no bridge across the ocean, and few hardy explorers had the resources, the courage, or the ships to venture on the journey. The first settlements in America, after those of the native Americans, were only about 400 years ago—practically yesterday in the scale of history. Those first settlers faced a bleak, desolate exis- ence in the new land and must often have longed for the comfort and security of their former homes in Europe. Some faltered and failed, but enough others had the faith and courage to stick it out, overcome hardships, and establish a "new world" in the Americas. Like them, we constantly face frightening unknowns in our own future, but we must build with confidence or perish in despair.

GARDENS

[242] On many a garden bench you'll find the words of Dorothy Frances Gurney, from her poem "The Lord God Planted a Garden," which read:

> The kiss of the sun for pardon,
> The song of the birds for mirth,
> One is nearer God's heart in a garden
> Than anywhere else on earth.

[243] Once I was given some seeds to plant in my garden. They looked like radish seeds, and that's what I thought I had planted.

I even made a little sign to place at the end of the row, RADISH. But what came up was kohlrabi. The little seeds knew what they were doing, even if I didn't.

[244] Soldiers stationed in the remote Aleutian island of Kiska were depressed by the bare landscape. The glacial rock supported little plant life, only a few tufts of grass, some hardy shrubs in the brief summer months, no trees. The camouflage unit undertook to remedy the situation. It constructed a tree from wire and canvas, attached some branches, glued on some plastic leaves. Then they put a fence around it with a sign saying, KISKA NATIONAL FOREST.

[245] Who plants a tree
Plants not what is, but is to be—
A hope, a thought for future years,
A prayer, a dream of higher things
That rise above our doubts and fears.
R. H. ADANS

GOALS

[246] Even when we do not achieve our goals, there is merit in striving toward them. On June 8, 1924, George Mallory and A. C. Irvine were close to their goal of reaching the top of Mount Everest. Others in their party watched from a camp 3500 feet below the peak. The two climbers ascended until they became two tiny black spots against the snow and sky. The last message they sent back was, "Going strong for the top." Mallory and Irvine disappeared from sight for a time, then emerged from the mists at the very top, and the watchers below knew they had conquered the mountain. Then a cloud blowing across the mountaintop hid them from sight, and that was the last ever seen of Mallory or Irvine. Without counting the cost, they had achieved their goal—"going strong for the top."

[247] Life's real satisfaction lies in setting and achieving a goal. How dull golf would be without the green, the theater without the final curtain, a sea voyage without a port, a poem without a last

line, a sermon without "Amen!" Anything left incomplete is frustrating. It's the end, the final achievement, that makes it worthwhile. For days and months to create a statue or painting an artist labors for the sake of the great day when he can sign it and call it complete. A musician gladly practices for hours and hours to achieve a perfect performance. The achievement of the goal makes all the difference, and the days spent working toward it become days of joy rather than days of drudgery.

[248] Aim at a barn door, and you'll never hit the weathercock on the steeple.

[249] When trolleys or trains ran on single tracks, one would have to switch over to a sidetrack to wait for others to pass. Some cars never seemed to get off the sidetrack; even today you can see rusting hulks of abandoned cars on some railroad sidings. Unfortunately this can happen in life, too. This was made meaningful to me by the story of a woman we'll call Marguerite. She attended a big funeral at the Roman Catholic cathedral in St. Louis. The mass lasted rather long, and she decided not to go to the cemetery.

However, as she got into her car and started out of the parking lot, the policeman who was arranging the funeral procession slapped a sticker on her car and ordered her to turn on the headlights. She started to explain but he wouldn't listen. "Lady, there are lots of cars behind you," he shouted. "Get into line please!" So she did, with half a hundred cars falling into line after her as they slowly started for the cemetery.

She kept thinking about how she could get out of the procession. Just ahead the big parking lot of Schnuck's Market came into view, and she decided this was her chance. As they passed the entrance to the parking lot, she turned her car out of line and into the lot—only to discover a moment later that every car behind her had followed!

Soon the policeman was back, and he was angry!

The story reminds me of how often we start out for somewhere and wind up in the parking lot at Schnuck's Market. Something gets us sidetracked, and then we have a hard time getting back on the right path again.

GOD'S LOVE

[250] A forest fire burned over some acreage near a farm in western Canada. Many of the farm's outbuildings were destroyed. When the embers had cooled, the farmer walked around looking over the ruins. Noticing one burned lump on the ground, he prodded it with his stick. It was a hen, burned to death. The farmer turned the hen over and, to his surprise, out ran three baby chicks, terrified and chirping. The hen had died in the flames, but somehow had saved her brood of chicks.

What a reminder of the promise of God's protecting love: "How often would I have gathered your children together as a hen gathers her brood under her wings, and you would not!" (Matt. 23:37)

[251] Remember the angel Gabriel in Marc Connelly's THE GREEN PASTURES? He was disgusted with human strife, waywardness, and sin and always wanted to blow his trumpet to end the world. But the Lord always restrained him. "Not yet, Gabe. Give them another chance." Remember that God's ways are not our ways, and be thankful.

[252] God is always doing things we don't expect and don't deserve. On a hot summer Sunday a minister was just starting his sermon when a loud clap of thunder was heard. A few minutes later the rain was pouring down. Said the minister to his congregation, "Isn't that just like God! Here we sit snug and dry, and he's out there washing our cars."

[253] A few years ago 236 people were killed in a Chicago plane crash. Most of us read about a disaster like that and shrug our shoulders. What does it really mean to us? But then we may read the list of casualties and find among them the name of a man who lived down the block on the very same street where we live, and suddenly the event strikes home. When we know someone or recognize someone, whatever happens to that person takes on a new meaning. That's why Jesus said that a good shepherd knows his sheep and is known by them. That's why God told the prophet, "I have called you by name, you are mine" (Isa. 43:1). That makes all the difference.

[254] The fact that God loves you doesn't come through logic but only through love. A child normally has no doubt about his mother's love, but this knowledge does not come through explanation. You can't tie a tot in a high chair and lecture to him about the meaning of love. Love is revealed by showing it, not by talking about it. The child in the home feels it, is sure of his place in the family, and knows that he counts as an individual—at least with his parents. Similarly, the assurance of God's love comes only because his spirit awakens it in our hearts.

[255] Madalyn Murray O'Hair is not the first atheist to gain great public attention on the American scene. Generations ago Robert Ingersoll drew large audiences for his lectures on atheism. He liked to shock his hearers by taking out a big pocket watch and announcing, "I give God—if there is one—five minutes to strike me dead." When someone called this to the attention of the English evangelist Joseph Parker, who was conducting revival meetings in America at the time, Parker responded with typical English aplomb: "And did the gentleman presume to exhaust the patience of the eternal God in five minutes?"

[256] The noted preacher Charles Haddon Spurgeon was once invited by a parishioner to visit his new house and barn. Spurgeon brought him a housewarming present, a weather vane with the motto, "God is love." The man asked, "Does that mean God's love is as changeable as the wind?"

Spurgeon replied, "No, indeed. It means that God is love whichever way the wind blows."

[257] An old woman in India turned to the Christian faith, making some of her unconverted neighbors furious. They shunned her at times and harrassed her, even shouting after her on the street. "You're the ugliest old woman I ever saw," one of them shouted.

She gently turned the attack aside. "Isn't it wonderful how God can love an ugly old woman like me!" she replied.

[258] "All persons are created equal" is the basis for democracy, but there has always been question about what equality means.

People are not equal in physical size or prowess. They're surely not equal in importance or in the value society places on their work. Starting salaries for a schoolteacher and a professional baseball player are startlingly different. Money and social standing are false measures. There's need to recognize the true values in life, the fact that every human being is precious in God's sight. Jesus dealt equally with all—rich, poor, employers, laborers, priests, kings, socialites, outcasts, prodigals, tax collectors, women, children, even a thief, and a traitor. He gave his life for them all.

GOD'S POWER

[259] In ancient times people thought of the universe as a little room with lights on the ceiling—big ones like the sun and moon and little ones like the stars. What was outside of this room, they could not even imagine. Today we know that our solar system is vast, and the solar system is only one little "corner" of the universe! There are stars 27 million times the size of our sun, and the edge of the known or suspected universe is 200,000 light years away —in miles that would be more than a quintillion, a one followed by 18 zeroes. And God rules it all. No wonder we can sing, "How great Thou art!"

[260] An artist took his aged father into his home. With feeble arthritic fingers the old man, also an artist, spent his days making little clay models. The results were crude, and the old man became depressed by the loss of his talents. At night, while the old man slept, his son took the clay models and with strong and skillful hands softened their lines and made them into things of beauty. In the morning the old man saw them and his heart was gladdened, though he never guessed the secret. Similarly, God takes our broken lives and our clumsy service and makes them perfect.

[261] God governs in the affairs of men, and if a sparrow cannot fall to the ground without his notice, neither can a kingdom rise without his aid.
BENJAMIN FRANKLIN

[262] A new boy moved into a crowded city block. He was a bully, and all the kids ran away and hid when he came around—all except one little youngster. The bully swaggered over to him and snarled, "What's the matter with you? Ain't you afraid of me?"

The youngster answered, "Course not. My big brother's the boxing champeen, and if you touch me he'll take you to pieces."

So the devil, the world, and our own flesh swagger up to us and demand, "Ain't you afraid?" But in Martin Luther's words we can answer, "No indeed! For us fights the Valiant One whom God Himself elected."

[263] Napoleon once seemed destined to conquer the world. He exalted his own power and commented that "God is always on the side of the heavy battalions." But eventually Napoleon was cut down to size and sent into exile. Victor Hugo remarked, "God got bored with him."

[264] Some great Christians have challenged God. In one of Martin Luther's prayers, he said, "Lord, this is your cause, not mine. Therefore do your own work, for if your gospel does not prosper, it will not be Luther alone who will be the loser, but your own name will be dishonored."

[265] The idea of partnership with God gives courage and peace. The coat of arms of the Netherlands illustrates this. It shows two clasped hands, one descended from above, the other reaching up from below. The motto on the coat of arms is "God Wills; I Can."

[266] God has power to turn tragedy into triumph. What appears to us to be a great defeat can sometimes be turned into a path to triumph. John Fletcher, whom John Wesley called "the holiest man into whose face I ever looked," had such an experience. An adventurous youth, Fletcher cared little for spiritual things. The lure of faraway places was in his blood. He joined the crew of a privateer which was sailing to America to rob Spanish ships of their gold. While his ship was docked at Lisbon, a clumsy servant spilled boiling water on Fletcher's leg. It would take a month to heal, so the captain of the privateer said, "We cannot wait; the ship will

sail without you." Fletcher counted it a tragedy as he watched the ship's sails disappear beyond the horizon, but the ship was never heard from again. Despondent, Fletcher went to England where he met the Wesleys and began a great career as a teacher and preacher. God had turned a possible tragic ending into a opportunity for a life of service.

[267] Bishop James Pike derided the concept of the Holy Trinity as a "committee god." On the other hand, Dr. James Reid said that we cannot say everything we mean by the word *God* until we say, "Father, Son, Spirit." For most of us the idea of the three-in-one is both baffling and yet helpful. It gives us three small windows into the eternal, a small glimpse of the incomprehensible power and majesty of God who could create us and all that exists.

[268] When a business establishment gets into financial trouble and has to be reorganized, the sign put out when it reopens for business usually say "Under New Management." This is intended as encouraging information for past customers and prospective clients, since it seems to indicate that things will be run better than before. There may be the same goods, the same staff, and the same work, but there's the promise of new methods, a new spirit, and better service. Like some business places, our lives can fail because they are badly managed. There's always a second chance, however. When we turn control over to God and live according to his laws, it can make life a divine adventure "under new management."

[269] An elderly lady was interviewed by reporters after she had survived an earthquake. "Weren't you afraid?" they asked.
"Not really," she replied. "I was kind of glad to know I have a God who can shake the world."

[270] People are sometimes bowed down under "life's crushing load," as Phillips Brooks calls it in a Christmas hymn, simply because they've never let God help them. There's an old stewardship slogan that says, if you need help, "Tell God and tell God's people."
A woman suffered from a nasal irritation for 10 years without complaining, but finally she mentioned her affliction to some

81

friends. They urged her to see a physician at a nearby clinic. When she did, in 10 minutes she had a salve to cure the condition. "Why in the world didn't you attend to it sooner?" the doctor asked.

"I never thought of asking anyone about it," she replied. We can find help from God or from God's people—but only when we admit our need.

GOD'S PRESENCE

[271] Two little girls wanted to go out for "trick or treat" on Halloween, insisting that they were grown-up enough to be safe even though it was dark. Their parents agreed to permit them to go. But as they went down the street, two figures followed after them, keeping in the shadows and trying to stay out of sight. Their fathers were going along to watch and guard, yet staying in the background in order not to destroy the youngsters' confidence in their ability to do it alone.

God is like that, always in the background, never interfering with our freedom, yet assuring our safety.

[272] No one can adequately picture God or describe him. Either is limiting, and God is limitless. Even the "him" is pure conjecture and used only for convenience. An ardent feminist might say, "Pray to God. She will help you." The Bible itself has problems when it tries to put God into finite terms. The psalmist saw God in a hundred forms—as a rock, a fortress, a mountain, a shepherd, a light, and many others. We may picture God as an old man seated on a throne because that's the way medieval artists showed him. Or we may think of God as a kindly old patriarch, exactly like the preacher in the next town. That's the way Roark Bradford depicted him in *Ol' Man Adam an' His Chillun*, the stories on which Marc Connelly based the play *The Green Pastures*. All such images are inadequate, yet all may help a little.

[273] An army officer was sent to Tibet on a dangerous mission. Two things he carried along with him gave him strength. The first was the knowledge that he had not undertaken the journey on his own but had been sent by a great power for a sound reason. The

second was that if he got into a tight place, his government would use all its resources to see him through safely. These are the same assurances God gives us all. He has placed us here for a good reason and promises to use all his resources to aid us. God is ready to see us through if we will only trust him.

[274] We need a chance to find God in daily life. The round of daily duties and the confusion and noise of the world make it difficult. How can we obey the psalmist's injunction to "Be still and know that I am God"? It's not easy, but some great souls have done it. For more than 60 years Brother Lawrence never lost the sense of God's presence. He was as conscious of God's nearness when he was cleaning pots and pans in the kitchen as he was when taking Communion at the altar. Charles Spurgeon claimed that he never spent 15 minutes without the consciousness of God and his nearness. God's presence can be with us wherever we are or whatever we do, if only we are conscious of it.

[275] Out for a walk with her father, a little girl came to the bank of a swift-flowing stream. There were pretty flowers at the edge of the stream and the girl wanted to pick some of them, but her father drew her back. He showed her that the running water had undercut the bank of the stream and made it unsafe. Disappointed, she persisted, "Daddy, how many flowers can I pick?"

"Pick as many as you can without letting go of my hand," her father answered.

That's a good rule for life. Whatever loosens our hold on the Master's hand should be deliberately avoided.

[276] Too often we turn our thoughts back to ancient times as though they had a special grace. A sentimental children's hymn still in use speaks of the "sweet story of old when Jesus was here among men . . . how I long to have been with him then." Søren Kierkegaard reminds us that this is not a sensible approach to the religion Jesus taught. If the presence of the physical body of Christ is so important, then the disciples had an unfair advantage over those of us who live 2000 years later. The early Christians would then be better than us simply because they were closer to the time of

Christ. As the historical Jesus fades farther into the mists of the past, he would then have less and less influence. For us, however, it is important to realize the presence of Christ today and to confront him in faith. We need, through the eyes of faith, to see Christ as a reality among us here and now!

[277] "What are you drawing?" a teacher asked a youngster.
"I'm drawing a picture of God," was the reply.
"But nobody knows what God looks like," the teacher protested.
"They will when I'm finished," said the child.

[278] David Livingstone, the African missionary-explorer, was received with silent respect and reverence by the commencement audience at Glasgow University, which conferred a doctorate on him. Gaunt and weary after 16 years in the African sun and 27 attacks of fever, with one arm made useless by the bite of a lion, Livingstone told the audience that he was going back to Africa. His work would be partly to open new trade routes, partly to help suppress the slave trade, and chiefly to seek new opportunities for the preaching of the gospel, he said. "Shall I tell you what has supported me through all these years of exile among people whose language I did not know and whose attitude toward me was often hostile and always uncertain?" he asked. "It was this: 'Lo, I am with you always even to the end of the world.'"

[279] Not too long ago prayer to God in heaven seemed simple. People believed the world was flat. Heaven was up above and hell was down below. Now it's not so simple any more. We know that what's above our heads now will be under our feet in 12 hours, as the world spins around. If God's in his heaven, is he up or down, far away or near at hand? Maybe we would do better to say that heaven is in God, or wherever God is. Actually, we are all in God—in whom we live and move and have our being.

[280] In the early days of the Communist revolution in Russia, a group of peasants met secretly for worship. During their meeting, police broke into the room and proceeded to take down the names of all who were present. They finished with 30 names and were

about to leave when one elderly peasant said, "One name is missing." The officer in charge took the roll again, but when he had finished the peasant said again, "One name is missing."

Impatiently the officer demanded, "Who is it? Tell me his name!"

The old peasant said, "Jesus Christ."

Muttering, "Oh, that's different," the police left the meeting, but the old peasant was right.

[281] Robert Dale, a popular preacher in Birmingham, England, was not the sort of person to suffer hallucinations. But as he was preparing an Easter sermon, he became vividly conscious of a presence in his study. It unnerved him, for he felt it must be the presence of Christ. He paced the floor in excitement, saying, "Jesus is living. He is here!" After that, every Sunday was Easter in his church. People thought he had misread the calendar, but he had instead found that his Lord was a living presence in his life.

GOD'S PROMISES

[282] The final book in the Old Testament canon, Malachi, scolds unfaithful priests and people but also carries some great promises.

On human compassion: "Have we not all one father? Has not one God created us? Why then are we faithless to one another, profaning the covenant of our fathers?" (2:10)

On stewardship: "Will man rob God? Yet you are robbing me. But you say, 'How are we robbing thee?' In your tithes and offerings. . . . Bring the full tithes into the storehouse, that there may be food in my house; and thereby put me to the test, says the Lord of hosts, if I will not open the windows of heaven for you and pour down for you an overflowing blessing" (3:8-10).

On hope: "For you who fear my name the sun of righteousness shall rise, with healing in its wings. You shall go forth leaping like calves from the stall. And you shall tread down the wicked, for they will be ashes under the soles of your feet, on the day when I act, says the Lord of hosts" (4:2-3).

[283] The Bible has many promises. Are they of any value? Well, look at a five-dollar bill and all you will see is a piece of paper with

some printing on it. What makes it valuable is the promise written or implied there. Bills now say they are "legal tender," which means that the government guarantees the amount printed on them. Formerly they said, "The United States of America will pay to the bearer on demand the sum of five dollars." In any event, it's only a promise, but on the strength of that promise you can buy things, or pay debts. Suppose you said, "It's only a promise. Throw this paper away!" You do not take this action because you believe the promise printed on the paper. Do you really think God's promises are less valid than the government's?

[284] A devout English judge in India befriended an Indian lad who came from a prominent family, but who had been cast out by his relatives because he had converted to Christianity. The judge took the boy into his household where he worked as a house boy or servant. It was the custom in the household to have devotions every evening, and one night the judge read the words, "Every one who has forsaken houses, brethren, wife, children or lands, for my name's sake, shall receive a hundredfold."

Turning to the lad, the judge said, "Nobody here has done this except Norbudur. Will you tell us, is it true?"

The Indian lad read the verse again, then said, "It says he gives hundredfold. I know he gives thousandfold."

[285] In the Sermon on the Mount, Jesus promised his disciples three things: that they would be entirely fearless, absurdly happy, and that they would get into trouble. They did get into trouble, and they found to their surprise that they were not afraid. They were absurdly happy, for they laughed over their own troubles and only cried over other people's.
W. R. MALTBY

GREED, SELFISHNESS

[286] Greed can be deadly. When the soldiers of Cortez invaded Mexico, they lusted for the Aztec treasures of gold, silver, and gems. In one battle the soldiers overpowered the poorly armed Aztecs and scooped up as much loot as they could carry, filling bags with

gold chains and jewelry. As the Spaniards fled, the Aztecs regrouped and pursued the robbers. Loaded down with heavy bags of gold, some of the Spaniards were quickly overtaken and killed. Only those who threw away most of their loot could escape.

[287] "Bitter Parent" wrote to a newspaper columnist to complain about his sons. He had educated them and cared for them, yet they and their wives had turned their backs on the old home and seldom visited it. The writer asked if all the work and money he had spent on his children was worthwhile. Such a letter arouses a certain sympathy, but the question arises whether the parent's love was really unselfish or whether the attention he demanded may not have been at the root of the situation. Affection is not bought with food or favors.

[288] Selfish people miss some of the best things in life. Seeking prominent places and personal rewards, they miss out on the joys of service and giving. "Look out for number one" is directly opposed to "Seek first his kingdom and his righteousness, and all these things shall be yours as well" (Matt. 6:33).

[289] A man once found a dollar bill in the street. Since then he's kept his eyes on the ground, always searching for more. He has accumulated 1,754 pins, 578 buttons, and $2.58—but he has lost the sight of the faces of friends, the loveliness of flowers, the glory of heaven and its blue skies.

[290] Two bachelor brothers lived together in a small Connecticut city. They stayed indoors most of the time, living as recluses, and no one dared come near their house. Both were university graduates, and they were reputed to be rich, but about once each week, dressed in moth-eaten old clothes, they walked together into the city and begged for food. Finally one died and the other became ill and unable to care for himself, so the local authorities responded to calls from neighbors and entered the house. The stench was nauseating, as they found dresser drawers and closets stuffed with food in various stages of decay. One room was stacked from floor to ceiling with newspapers and magazines. As they proceeded to burn

some of the papers, fragments of paper money were found in the fire. A search through the rest of the papers turned up thousands of dollars. Those two old men had carried to the extreme the common human failing of acquiring possessions and trusting in them.

[291] Human nature sometimes leads us to believe that God wants us to have the biggest and best, so we might as well take it for ourselves. We are like a little boy who was offered some cake. There were two pieces on the plate, a big one and a little one, so the boy said, "I'm sure my little sister would like a piece. May I give her one?"

The adults in the room were deeply moved by this graciousness and commented on how polite the little boy was. But one of them said to the boy, "You're not usually so thoughtful about your sister. How come?"

The boy answered honestly, "Well, if I took the first piece, I'd have to take the little one, so I offered it to her first so she'd have to take the little one and leave the big one for me."

GROWTH

[292] A rural church had one member who insisted he was the best Christian in town but who rarely attended services, never did much, never knew much, never gave much. The minister kept after him, urging him to grow in faith, but he had one consistent answer: "Preacher, I may not seem to make much progress, but my faith is firmly established."

Then one spring day when he was hauling a heavy load of logs, his truck got stuck in the mud at the side of the road and couldn't budge. Just then the minister came by and couldn't resist the opportunity to remark, "Well, brother, I see you're not making much progress, but you are surely firmly established!"

Don't be stuck in the mud. Grow!

[293] In the spring of 1945, Allied forces made a great advance through Germany. One detachment of tanks raced ahead, then suddenly stopped. Headquarters contacted them by radio to demand the reason. "We have come to the edge of the map," they replied. Their

campaign map showed them the route they were to take, but they had raced ahead so rapidly that they came to the end of the map and were uncertain how to proceed. Some people reach the end of their map rather quickly, and it becomes a tragedy because their sympathies narrow and they can see only what's in their immediate vicinity. We need bigger maps, better plans, and a broader view.

[294] An old Philadelphia church proclaims, "Our endowment funds insure the existence of our church for all time." That's unfortunate and maybe tragic. That church could be like a mummy, all wrapped up in government bonds and dead as a doornail, existing always, whether it was useful or not. "Pay as you go" may be risky, but it's closer to the gospel. Life and growth are a daily necessity.

GUIDANCE

[295] Travelers know the value of road signs. Sometimes the signs may be misleading, but without them how confused most of us would be. In 1940 all street signs and direction markers were removed from the roads of England because of the fear of invasion. Soon afterward, however, they were restored because so many American soldiers were getting lost.

[296] Clear thinking demands concentration. Henry Thoreau, who lived in a much quieter age, found it necessary to seek the undisturbed silence of a remote pond where he could push his boat out from the shore and be completely alone, surrounded by quiet. But Horace Greeley used to sit on the porch of the old Astor House in New York, with the clatter of Broadway traffic sweeping by, writing deep, clear editorials. In the commotion and chatter of a newsroom, reporters turn out brisk and clear articles amid a thousand distracting noises. The secret is to concentrate—to withdraw from the turmoil around you and confront your immediate problems no matter where you are.

[297] Our generation is not accustomed to doing its own thinking. Opinions come to us ready-made from commentators, editorial writ-

ers, or propagandists. We quote others, but rarely ourselves. So many voices surround us each day from television, radio, newspapers, magazines, movies, neighbors, and even from chance acquaintances, that we rarely have time to think for ourselves. We tend to become like the old man, rocking away on his porch, who said, "Sometimes I sit and think, but most times I just sit."

[298] God does not perform a miracle when other means are at hand. Don't look for handwriting on the wall or listen for voices from heaven. God leads people in subtle ways that they usually cannot explain. They'll say, "I had a feeling." "I just couldn't get it out of my mind." "I just felt moved to do it." God leads us quietly, gently, step by step, one day at a time. He may not brilliantly light up the whole countryside for our benefit, but it's enough that he lights up the road right in front of us.

[299] Driving on a strange road, you may see a signpost that says, "To Centerville." You may check your map and find that there is indeed a road that goes to Centerville. You have never seen Centerville or been on the road before, but you may still drive along it rather confidently. The map and the signpost must be right, and eventually you'll get to Centerville. That's a form of faith, and on the road of life we can proceed only by faith.

[300] A sailor adrift at sea on a dark night faces danger from shoals, reefs, rocks, and unfriendly winds. If his compass isn't working and his charts are inadequate, he may circle about in confusion. Some people sail like that along the sea of life, circling about in dizzying uncertainty. But when that mariner has something to guide him, even a faint star or a distant lighthouse, he can set his course firmly and courageously. So on the sea of life, we need some light to guide us. God's Word is such a light, says the psalmist.

[301] Occasionally we're tempted to say that we don't need moral guidance in life, that we can work out our own destiny. But trusting in human values is never safe, and we are likely to wind up on the rocks. The U.S. Navy provided a comic example of this some years ago when the huge battleship *Missouri*, during routine ma-

neuvers, ran hard aground. It had 3000 trained men aboard, every possible navigating device, equipment that told the depth of the water under the bow and the ship's exact position. It was equipped to sail through fog or darkness as confidently as through clear daylight. Yet on a calm, bright, sunny morning it ran aground on a sandbar because human judgment had failed. Some channel markers had been moved from the place where they were supposed to be, and no one was alert enough to discover the error. While the result was more ludicrous than tragic, it warns us that life based only on human abilities is shaky and dangerous.

[302] After World War II some lighthouse keepers off the coast of Scotland spied a huge mine drifting toward their shore. They watched with fatal fascination as each wave brought it a little closer. They could do nothing to prevent it from being washed onto their beach, but they took what precautions they could to protect the light. Shortly afterward, people in a nearby village heard a great explosion. Some venturesome fishermen sailed out toward the lighthouse to find out what had happened. They found one of the keepers severely injured and a gaping hole where the mine had struck against rocks and exploded. But the light? It shone on undamaged to guide mariners safely to port. Sometimes we feel that total war and disaster is drifting closer and closer to us, while we can do little to stop it. But we can make sure that the light of love and truth keeps on shining.

GUILT, FORGIVENESS

[303] Guilt gives us no rest until it is forgiven and wiped out. A quiet, honorable man was fingerprinted for security reasons at the factory where he worked. He was a respected citizen, a faithful and devoted father. Everyone was shocked when a few months later some government agents came to the town with a warrant for his arrest. "You are wanted for a murder in Colorado 20 years ago," they said.

In dejection and fear the man went with them, for the secret that he had suppressed for 20 years had caught up with him. Later he said, "I'm glad. It's haunted and tortured me for all these years even though I changed my name and tried to live openly, thinking I was safe from detection." His fine record helped him, and in the subsequent trial he pleaded self-defense. The jury believed him, so he became a free man for the first time in all those years. True peace of mind comes only when we stop trying to hide guilt but instead expose it to the light of day and the hope of forgiveness.

[304] Never be ashamed to ask forgiveness. If you ask it of an adversary, you honor his sense of justice and mercy. If you ask it of God, it has already been granted, because only a repentant heart would lead you to seek it. God wants to forgive us, and we should be willing to be forgiven.

[305] Martin Luther recorded an imaginary conversation in which the devil said to him, "Luther, you are a great sinner and you will be damned."

Luther replied, "But that is not good reasoning. It is true that I am a great sinner, but it is written that Jesus Christ came to save sinners. Therefore I shall be saved."

[306] Swimming with a group of boys, one youngster went out far beyond his depth and began to panic and cry for help. A lifeguard quickly swam out to rescue him, but the boy in his terror struggled and kicked against his rescuer. Finally the lifeguard had to hit him hard enough to quiet him down so he could be towed ashore. I don't like to suggest that God does that to us, but it emphasizes the point that our own struggles may work against us. Only when we are able to relax and yield our own way and give ourselves over to God can he help us.

[307] A man trying to get rid of a big dog took the dog out in a boat and pushed him overboard in an attempt to drown him. As he struggled to push the dog out of the boat, the man lost his balance and fell into the water. A poor swimmer, he thrashed about until the dog jumped in, took hold of his collar, and pulled him safely to shore.

[308] Governor James Oglethorpe of Georgia had an argument

with a servant and ordered the man deported and sent back to England. "I never forgive disobedience," he said.

When John Wesley heard of it, he told the governor, "Then, sir, I hope you never sin!"

In a similar incident, King George IV of England wanted to receive Holy Communion and became very angry when the servant who brought the bishop was late. The king severely rebuked the servant and ordered him dismissed, then said to the bishop, "Now, your Grace, proceed with the Communion." Mildly but firmly, the bishop refused. Finally the king understood and said, "You are right. Call back the servant."

[309] Like old cuts and scars, old grudges between people or between nations cause constant irritations. If you have a grudge, get rid of it before it gets rid of you. Forgiveness is essential to life.

[310] A clergyman appealed to a wealthy friend on behalf of a worthy cause. The friend listened to the presentation, then produced a checkbook and signed a check, but left the amount blank. "Take this and fill it in," he told the clergyman. "I'll be good for whatever amount you choose."

Taking the check, the minister stammered his thanks but left the man's office in a mental turmoil. How should he fill it in? Too small an amount might be an insult to his friend's generosity, but dare he write in thousands of dollars of someone else's money? He was torn by doubts and struggled and prayed over the problem for a day or more. Finally he made his decision. He wrote in a high amount that he felt was indicative of the giver's generosity, but then he took the check back to his wealthy friend and showed it to him. "I put down a high amount to make it worthy of your generous spirit," he said.

If this seems an unlikely story, apply it to forgiveness. Every time we pray the Lord's Prayer, we ask God to accept what we have filled in on the check. "Forgive us," we pray, "as we forgive."

[311] Most people are rightfully irritated when dinner guests prowl around the kitchen or poke into closets. We all have some dusty old things we'd rather not have people see. It's the same in our

lives. Too often there are hidden fears, grudges, or guilt that we tuck away into the basement of our souls, hoping that nobody ever finds them out. Yet the only sure way to avoid this is to clean up those dusty old things and bring them out into the light. Who knows, maybe some broken old toy may turn out to be a valuable antique!

HAPPINESS

[312] Happiness does not come through material things or possessions. A fabled king learned that lesson. He was unhappy and asked a wise man how to find happiness. Find the happiest man in your kingdom," the sage advised. "Then borrow his shirt and wear it." So the king searched throughout his kingdom and finally found a woodcutter who seemed supremely happy. The king explained the reason for his search and then asked the woodcutter for his shirt—but the man didn't own a shirt! Thus the truth dawned upon the king, that possessions or position do not necessarily bring happiness.

[313] He who joy would win
Must share it. Happiness
Was born a twin.
LORD BYRON

[314] Three enemies of happiness are worry, boredom, and selfishness. Worry hangs like a sword of Damocles over our heads, keeping us uneasy and unable to move because we are paralyzed by cares. Boredom keeps us plodding through life, head down, nothing to sing about, nothing to praise. Selfishness turns us inward, interested in nothing but ourselves.

Religious faith restores happiness because it overcomes these enemies. Why worry? God is on the throne, and, if all else fails, underneath are God's everlasting arms. Why be bored? Life is full of wonder and creativity and bursting horizons, both in nature and in knowledge. How dare you be selfish? Life is to be lived for others, and love can lift you out of your narrow self and send you forth to serve.

[315] It is agreed by all, I think, that the two happiest periods of a man's life are his boyhood and about 10 years from now.
EUGENE WOOD

[316] "Happiness is a warm puppy," according to Charles M. Schultz. That's a much simpler definition than is given by the poet William Wordsworth, who asks, "Who is the happy Warrior? Who is he/That every man in arms should wish to be?" Then in 78 lines of poetry, Wordsworth sets so many conditions that you wonder if anyone could fill his definition of what it means to be happy. The happy warrior achieves "the plan that pleased his boyish thought"; he is "diligent to learn"; he travels in company with pain, fear, and bloodshed but turns "this necessity to glorious gain"; although exposed to suffering and distress "he is alive to tenderness"; and he's always giving birth to noble deeds. Fortunately we do not have to live by such farfetched poetic definitions. When we have food, shelter, friends, and the knowledge that God loves us, we are all warm puppies.

[317] One rainy day someone said, "What miserable weather!" But the next morning as I stood at the window looking out, I saw a big fat robin using a puddle of water for a bathtub—splashing, gurgling, fluttering, and thoroughly enjoying himself in that heaven-sent bath. When our heavenly Father cares so much for one of the least of his creatures, should we ever be gloomy or discouraged?

HOPE

[318] My heart leaps up when I behold
A rainbow in the sky.
WILLIAM WORDSWORTH

[319] If all my ships go out to sea
And never one comes home to me;
If I must watch day after day
By empty waters cold and gray;
Then I shall fashion one ship more
From bits of driftwood on the shore.

I'll build that ship with toil and pain
And send it out to sea again.
ANONYMOUS

[320] Martin Luther in his later years was subject to periods of melancholy and depression. One day he seemed particularly gloomy, so his wife Catherine von Bora dressed herself up in mourning clothes of black crepe. When Luther demanded to know why she was in mourning, she said, "I thought God died." Luther got the message.

[321] When they're at the end of their rope, beaten, exhausted, and desolate, the Germans say they're at "the last chapter of Matthew." It's an expression interpreted to mean the end of everything, when despair takes over. But if you look at that last chapter of Matthew, you find in its closing words a splendid hope, for Jesus says, "Lo, I am with you always, to the close of the age."

[322] An angel paused in its onward flight
With a seed of love and truth and light
   And cried, "Oh where can this seed be sown
That it will be most fruitful when grown?"
   The Savior heard and said as he smiled,
"Place it for me in the heart of a child."

[323] Speak about the parable of the great supper in the Bible, Pope Gregory the Great said, "Man's desire for heavenly things is so faint that God graciously presents these things to him under the inviting and alluring images of a banquet, so that he may be stirred up to a more earnest longing after them."

[324] Partings are often sad. Dryden wrote, "Parting is worse than death; it is the death of love." Shakespeare adds, "Farewell! God knows when we shall meet again./I have a faint, cold fear thrills through my veins,/That almost freezes up the heat of life." He even agonizes over lovers' parting: "Parting is such sweet sorrow/That I shall say good night till it be morrow." Every air terminal or ship's dock is a daily witness to the tears of parting; and the deepening

shadows of approaching death bring sadness. But when Jesus parted from the disciples for the last time on the Day of Ascension, they returned to Jerusalem with great joy, praising and blessing God. When faith takes over, sorrow gives way to joy.

HUMILITY

[325] Robert Burns was plowing a field one November, either actually or in his imagination. As he plowed, he turned up a nest of field mice. He picked up a "wee, sleekit, cow'rin, tim'rous beastie" and philosophized over her long hours of labor building the nest, a cozy place of moss and grass, now destroyed beyond repair.
"But, mousie, thou art no thy-lane,
in proving foresight may be vain;
The best laid schemes o' mice an' men,
Gang aft agely, And leave us nought but grief and pain
For promis'd joy!"
We build up our comfortable little worlds, fence them in, and think they are permanent, but then fate draws some giant plow through them. "Humility is the solid foundation of all the virtues," said Confucius.

[326] A gifted violinist who played with the Philadelphia Orchestra sent her young daughter to study violin under the tutelage of a stranger, a much less talented person. She said, "I would like to teach her myself, but I must wait until she asks. I cannot impart these things to her until she is ready to receive them." Often such relationships exist between parents and children. Parents may have the knowledge, but they cannot force it on their children and must wait until the children are ready to listen and to receive. Something similar exists between us and God. God often wants to give us grace and love and forgiveness, but he cannot do so until we admit our need and are ready to receive. When we discover our own helplessness and humbly acknowledge it, God can give us his help.

[327] To see ourselves as we are is difficult. People have their picture taken by a good photographer, then look at the proofs and

say, "That's not a good likeness." But the camera isn't lying. It reflects what it sees. What these people really mean is, "The picture is not flattering enough."

[328] There's a saying in the legal profession that "a person who acts as his own lawyer has a fool for a client." While that may be simply an effort by lawyers to enrich themselves at the expense of others, there are many things we cannot do for ourselves. A surgeon cannot operate on himself; a dentist cannot fill his own teeth; a barber cannot cut his own hair. Whether we like it or not, we are dependent on others for many things.

[329] An architect complained that people ask him to design a house and then come to him with the plans for it already in mind, simply expecting him to rubber-stamp his approval. We do that often in our lives. We make our own plans and then come to God asking that they be sanctioned.

[330] One of the first Russian satellites bore a "crew" of two specially trained monkeys. Later many men and women soared through space and even walked on the moon, but in suitable humility we ought to remember that the monkeys got there first!

[331] It is difficult for us to admit our own emptiness and impotence, but only when we do so can power flow into us and through us. Did you ever think of the importance of a vacuum? A vacuum has great power because its emptiness can attract things to it. The principle of a vacuum operates cleaning devices, electric bulbs, thermometers, and similar instruments, and even makes it possible for a jet plane to fly.

[332] God excludes no one, but sometimes people shut themselves out of his kingdom of love. This was brought home to me by an incident at the post office. A woman had a package and tried to push it through the window to the clerk, but it wouldn't go. She turned it sidewise, but still it would not fit through the window. Finally the harried clerk said to her, "Lady, I guess you just made the package too big."

This applies to God's kingdom, too. People are puffed up, infatuated with their own importance, sure of their own righteousness, and as a result they make themselves too big for the kingdom. A contrite, humble, believing heart is all that's needed. God shuts no one out, but our own inflated egos may shut God out of our lives.

[333] A little learning can lead to arrogance, but a great deal of learning leads to humility. Human beings who thought they knew all the answers often went forth boldly, only to come back sadder and wiser. Bankers and brokers thought they knew all about money, but many went bankrupt in the crash of 1929. Because he did not know the lessons of history, Adolf Hitler boasted that only he was fit to rule the world. You can go on with the list indefinitely!

[334] Nobody knows how many stars are in the heavens, but the number—if you'll pardon the expression—is astronomical. A single galaxy may have a hundred billion stars, and there are hundreds of millions of galaxies. Although we can see only about 6000 stars on a clear night, the total number of stars are countless. Many are in the Milky Way, which Joyce Kilmer dubbed "Main Street, Heaventown." Before smog and city lights dimmed our vision, the brightness of the stars intrigued people who felt that every movement in the heavens had some omen. The ancient superstition of astrology developed and still influences people today. In a more practical way, the stars made navigation possible, guiding the Phoenicians and Greeks and Norsemen on their voyages, helping Columbus, Magellan, and every other venturesome mariner to find his way. In all ages the vast silences of space have reminded people of their human frailty as well as of the immense majesty of God.

[335] A minister visited at the sick bed of a prominent jurist, and they talked for a while in a learned way about important issues of the day. Then the judge said, "Pardon me, but you know that I'm facing real things. Won't you talk to me plainly about what I need to hear?"

The pastor quietly said, "You're a sinner, like me. Jesus died for our sins. Put your trust in him like a little child."

The judge responded, "Thank you. I can get hold of that."

IMMORTALITY

[336] John Brashear was a grinder of lenses for telescopes and an astronomer of note as well as a kindly, cheerful man. Over his grave in Pittsburgh, Pennsylvania, is inscribed this couplet:

Though my soul may set in darkness, it will rise in perfect light.
I have loved the stars too dearly to be fearful of the night.

[337] Anyone who loves a garden or who works with the soil has a vision of immortality. In northern climes autumn days and early frosts cause the leaves to turn brown and fall, the flowers to wilt and die. But no gardener burns his tools and says, "That's all there is." The gardener instead clears away the debris and goes home to peruse his seed catalogs. Then in spring the brown turns to green once more, and the flowers bloom again. The German poet Goethe rightly said, "In springtime all nature preaches immortality."

[338] A skeptic once teased a Christian friend by asking, "Say, George, what would you say if, after you die, you found there wasn't such a place as heaven after all?"

With a smile, the believer replied, "I would say, well, I've had a good time getting there anyway." Then he added, "Say, Fred, what would you say if, when you die, you found there was such a place as hell after all?"

[339] Life is always too short. If Methuselah really lived 969 years, he probably left this world still feeling that there was much undone. But when someone is cut down in the prime of youth, the tragedy is compounded. John Milton calls death "the blind Fury with th' abhorréd shears,/Who slits the thin-spun life." When Cecil Rhodes lay dying at the age of 49 after a life of great achievement and high adventure, his words were, "So little done, so much to do." It is typical for us humans to plead for more time, for whenever death comes we say, "Not yet! There is still so much to do."

[340] In the days of King Louis XIV of France, a court physician or astrologer—for the two professions were then related—foretold the death of one of the king's favorites. The king thought the lady's

death was the fault of the astrologer and called him in with the intention of ordering him executed. "What can you tell me about your own death?" the king asked.

The astrologer replied, "Your Majesty, I perceive that I will die three days before you do." The king believed him and from that time on was very careful about the astrologer's health.

[341] Bombed twice, St. Philip's Church in London was left after World War II as a roofless, burned-out shell. Broken fragments were used to rebuild the walls and restore the building to use. At the rededication of the church, a poem was read:
"There lives a beauty that men cannot kill;
Yea, that shall kill all ugliness at last,
For Christ in love's white vesture walks with us still.
Hold that truth and hold it fast!"

[342] An old legend tells of a parish priest who found a branch of a thorn tree twisted around so that it resembled a crown of thorns. Thinking it a symbol of the crucifixion of Christ, he took it into his chapel and placed it on the altar on Good Friday. Early on Easter morning he remembered what he had done. Feeling it was not appropriate for Easter Sunday, he hurried into the church to clear it away before the congregation came. But when he came into the church, he found the thorn branches blossoming with beautiful roses.

[343] In *The Woman of Andros* Thornton Wilder tells a story that he later incorporated into the great play *Our Town*. The gods granted a dead youth the privilege of returning to his home to relive one day of his life. His mother glanced at him and went on with her work without speaking. His father passed him by unseeing, for his mind was full of daily cares and problems. The youth then realized that "the living, too, are dead and we can only be said to be alive in those moments when our hearts are conscious of their treasure." How often this can apply to us as we pass by one another like shadows because we are wrapped up in our own self-centered lives!

[344] "Some morning you will read in the papers that Dwight L. Moody is dead," the famed evangelist once told a group of friends. "Don't believe a word of it. At that moment I shall be more alive than I am now. I was born in the flesh in 1837. I was born in the spirit in 1856. That which is born of the flesh may die; that which is born of the spirit shall live forever."

[345] In 1728 Benjamin Franklin composed this epitaph for himself: "The body of Benjamin Franklin, Printer (like the cover of an old book, its contents torn out and stripped of its lettering and gilding), lies here, food for worms; but the work shall not be lost, for it will (as he believed) appear once more in a new and more elegant edition, revised and corrected by the Author."

[346] A million years from now, you and I, looking back on this present time with its light afflictions which are but for a moment, will see it in its right relation to the life beyond; and it will seem as far away and as faint as the glimmer of the remotest of the fixed stars in the heavens. Then we will wonder at the hold that the seen and the temporal had on us; for our life will be arched over by the unseen and eternal, and we shall understand at last the true meaning of life—life that lasts forever, and ever, and ever.
D. James Burrell

INDIFFERENCE

[347] You can't please everybody. No matter how much you try to please, some people are never going to love you—a notion that troubles at first but is eventually relaxing. Most people are neither for you or against you but rather are thinking about themselves.
John W. Gardner

[348] Usually we speak of a person who stands aside and watches events as an "innocent bystander." Giving a new twist to this phrase, TV commentator Roderick MacLeish wrote a book entitled, *The Guilty Bystander*. It has been well said that all that's necessary for evil to triumph is for good people to do nothing.

[349] Nothing is more pathetic than a neglected cemetery, where stones are toppled and weeds grow unchecked. It seems obvious that nobody cares. As a visitor to Paris I stood near the famed Arch of Triumph, watching the crowds hurry by. Atop the arch a flickering flame burned in honor of all France's war casualties, but nobody paid attention. Not a hat was lifted, not a second glance was given. No wonder Jeremiah cried, "Is it nothing to you, all you who pass by?" (Lam. 1:12). On Calvary, an innocent person gave his life as a sacrifice for the world, but throughout the ages many have simply passed by unheeding.

[350] There are two ways to lose our liberty. One is to have it taken away forcibly by those who seek their own ends and desire power above all else. "Eternal vigilance is the price of liberty" as we remain alertly on guard against those who oppose our freedom and would like to gain power over us. The other way to lose liberty is by indifference. Our ancestors fought and bled for the right to vote, but even in our most important elections a large percentage of the citizenry does not bother to go to the polls. Our ancestors fought and bled for the right to worship according to their conscience, but millions disregard this right and ignore the open doors of the churches.

[351] The straight and narrow path might not be so narrow if more people walked on it.

[352] A townhouse in a crowded Los Angeles suburb was the scene of gruesome murders. Three people were executed and dismembered in a bloody orgy, probably drug-related. Police came upon the bodies by accident, having been alerted by a postman who wondered why mail wasn't being picked up. In an effort to reconstruct the crime, police questioned neighbors about unusual noises they might have heard. Several neighbors said they had heard screams and yells and were even able to pinpoint the exact time. They said there had often been noisy parties at the house, with yelling and screaming, so that they did not suspect that a crime was being committed. They also claimed that when they reported the noisy parties to the

police, the police rarely bothered to respond. The whole event was typical of a city where nobody cares much.

[353] In some countries people salute one another on Easter by saying, "Christ is risen." The response is, "Christ is risen indeed." It's a common salutation, just as we greet one another with "Happy Easter" without thinking much about the religious implications of the festival.

One Easter Sunday a man attended an inspiring service at which this salutation was explained and used. He left the church determined to spread the message. To the first person he met on the street, he issued the salutation, "Christ is risen!"

The person looked back at him blankly, responding, "Huh? What did you say?"

INDIVIDUALS

[354] Your own life may seem to be pulled in a thousand directions, weighed down by burdens, fears, prejudices, ambitions, and conflicting desires. At times there are so many pieces that life becomes like a jigsaw puzzle with little meaningless pieces scattered all over. How can you restore it to a meaningful pattern? In *The Dark Night of the Soul* Georgia Harkness gives her personal testimony as an answer: "The Christian faith imparts meaning to life. A living faith that is centered in God as revealed in Christ takes our chaotic, disorganized selves, with their crude jumble of pleasures and pains, and knits them together into a steadiness and joy that can endure anything with God."

[355] Great things are not accomplished by masses, but always by individuals. Ben Franklin, flying a kite, found electricity in the atmosphere. An individual made this discovery. It did not come into the world in a vague way, reaching everyone, but came through an individual mind. Louis Pasteur saw a man's leg being burned in order to clear up an infection, and this led him to great discoveries about antiseptics and the control of bacteria. With these and many other great discoveries, an individual was responsible.

104

[356] After Dwight L. Moody's Chicago church burned down, he went to London. He preached there one Sunday morning, and his message fell flat. It failed so miserably that he felt he had nothing to offer an English congregation, and he didn't want to preach again. He spent much of the afternoon in prayer, wrestling with his conscience. In the evening the powers of an unseen world fell on his audience and more than 500 responded to his appeal that they make Christ the master of their lives. What happened in between? No individual can accomplish much alone, but one individual plus God can work miracles!

[357] Every individual has an important part to play in life. No one is so small or insignificant that he or she doesn't count. A tooth is a small thing. An adult may have 32 teeth in his mouth. Each tooth weighs only about one ounce or 1/24th of one percent of the average body. Yet if it misbehaves, how that one little tooth can affect the whole body! It makes you realize the importance of just one little member.

[358] Uncle Sam says that in any correspondence about taxes I must identify myself by my Social Security number. My bank says that my checks will not be honored unless I put my account number on them. The company that sells me gasoline says, "Be sure to include your account number in any correspondence." Another company sends me a buff-colored card with little holes in it and says it can recognize me only if I present that card. Everywhere the world seems determined to impress on me that I am a number or a hole in a computer card! The only place where I can be sure that I am an individual, different from everyone else and respected for myself, is when I stand before God. He said, "I have called you by name, you are mine" (Isa. 43:1).

INFLUENCE

[359] A woman said to me, "I just don't understand it. My husband never came to church, and every week I would scold and scold. Then I just gave him up for lost and never mentioned it again. Now he comes every week. Why?"

[360] Rider Haggard's mother brought up seven sons without ever raising her voice to them. She explained, "With seven noisy boys in the house, shouting would not do a bit of good. I found that a whisper was much more effective."

[361] Outdoor advertising illumination was not widely used in 1918, but when New York churches were closed because of the ravaging epidemic of influenza, one minister arranged to have spotlights placed inside his church so that its magnificent stained-glass windows would be lighted and would give passersby the full effect of the pictures. Seen from outside the church, the eloquent sermons in glass attracted more attention than the minister's regular sermons. People came from all over the city to tarry reverently outside the church and then to leave with renewed confidence.

[362] Paul became the most vital man in the Roman Empire. Men might have resisted his arguments, but they could not resist the light in his eye, the triumph in his face, the joy in his voice, the dauntless courage of his activity.
LYNN HAROLD HOUGH

[363] Visitors to Florence, Italy, troop to the Church of Santa Croce to view the burial place of the famed artist Michelangelo. As they walk across the floor to his tomb, they cross a stone slab set into the floor. The traffic of centuries has worn away the inscription on that slab, but it marks the burial place of Domenico Ghirlandajo, Michelangelo's art teacher. The teacher did his work well and the fame of his disciple far exceeded that of the teacher himself, although Ghirlandajo was a great artist in his own right. But for most tourists, the teacher's grave is unnoticed, while the pupil's is honored.

[364] An artist painted a picture of wintry twilight, showing trees laden with snow and a dreary, dark house, lonely and desolate. It was a moving scene, but a sad one. Then the painter added a stroke of golden yellow paint. It made a window seem lighted, with the light streaming out across the snow. The effect was magical. A sad

scene was transformed into one of comfort and good cheer. "So shines a good deed in a naughty world," as Shakespeare puts it.

INTEGRITY

[365] Many years ago when sports were less professional and more fun, Grantland Rice immortalized the true spirit of sportsmanship in a poem that included the lines,

> When the One Great Scorer comes to write against your name—
> He marks—not that you won or lost—but how you played the game.

Either those words are rank nonsense, or they embody a timeless truth. With today's emphasis on winning at all costs, they are often overlooked. But they are true.

[366] For many years a man had worked faithfully as foreman of the building crew for a wealthy contractor. The contractor decided to take a long vacation on a world cruise, but before leaving he gave his foreman a set of plans for a dream house. "Build it according to specifications and spare no expense," he instructed. "I want this to be a good house for a special reason."

After the contractor had gone, the foreman thought about the many years he had worked for small wages, and he decided that this was the time to make a profit for himself. He cut down on the specifications for the house and substituted cheap material wherever it would not show, pocketing the difference. Then the contractor returned and examined the house. Then he told the foreman, "You have served me well for many years. In reward I have planned this house for you. It is yours, to own and live in."

Who got cheated?

[367] The Great Wall of China was a wonder of the ancient world. It stretched 1500 miles, cost huge amounts of money and thousands of lives, and took many years to build. Although it was a formidable defense system, enemies penetrated the wall three times during the first few years of its existence. They did it not by knocking holes in the wall, or climbing over it, but by the simple expedient

of bribing the gatekeepers. The Great Wall was no stronger than the character of those who kept its gates.

[368] Two brave and bold knights met under a huge shield. One, astride his horse on one side of the shield, said the shield was made of silver. The other, on the other side, said it was gold. The argument grew hot and finally they drew their lances and faced off against one another. In the course of their joust, their positions were reversed, and, to their chagrin and astonishment, they discovered that it was indeed gold on one side but silver on the other. The whole truth is often not only on one side.

[369] Four things that we must learn to do
If we would make our record true:
To think without confusion clearly,
To act from honest motives purely,
To love our fellowmen sincerely,
To trust in God and man securely.

[370] An old legend tells of a beloved prince who invited all his friends to come to his birthday party, asking each to bring a bottle of his best wine. A barrel was placed at the palace door, and each person on entering was to pour the wine into the container, as a symbol of the blending of their love and loyalty for the prince. One guest looked over his stock of choice wines and found it hard to part with even one bottle. He thought, "I will fill a bottle with water and pour it into the barrel. With all that good wine, nobody will notice the difference." The prince was pleased with his gifts and when he was shown the big barrel, he wept with joy and invited all the guests to gather around and drink to his health. He held up a wine glass and turned on the spigot—but all that came from the barrel was water!

[371] We're inclined to glamorize things that were really rather sordid. At Christmas time we sing about the manger, as if this were a thing of beauty. It was far from it, as anyone who has ever been in a stable can easily testify. And we shape crosses out of gold and other precious metal and adorn them with jewels, as if the cross

were something splendid. Quite the contrary, it was the gallows or electric chair or gas chamber of its day, providing a tortured death for outcasts from society.

[372] The son of Scipio Africanus, a noted Roman general, wore a signet ring with his father's picture on it. His life was dissolute, worthless, and harmful, so finally the Roman senate forbade him to wear the ring because he was a disgrace to his father. As God's children, how do we match up?

[373] Four boys found $13,000 in a brown paper bag on a New York street. Three of the boys wanted to divide the money and keep it. The fourth one persuaded them that the honest thing to do was to inform the police. The police took the money, but the boys' action was widely publicized. In no time at all, a dozen claimants showed up to state that the money was theirs. It's amazing how many people lose $13,000 in a brown paper bag! After a period of time had elapsed, the case was brought before the court, and the boys were called in. The judge listened to all the claimants, then praised the boys' honesty and awarded the money to them. Faced with a conflict of right or wrong, they had made the right choice.

[374] One curse of formal religion is that it makes people say things they don't really mean. The Lord's Prayer, for instance, is solemnly repeated at church services, schools, assemblies, and all sorts of meetings. "Forgive us our sins as we forgive those who sin against us," people blandly repeat, believing they are asking God to forgive them when in truth they may be asking God to strike them down. If God forgave us only in the grudging and limited way we forgive others, we'd be doomed. Only the limitless patience of the merciful God gives us chance after chance.

[375] A Brooklyn church faced calamity when its $400,000 mortgage came due. An aggressive financial campaign had raised only $100,000. The bank that held the mortgage refused the $100,000 and foreclosed its mortgage. But what can a bank do with a church building? They put it on the market. Then the congregation

changed its name and bought the building back for $400,000, making a down payment of $100,000 and leaving the other $300,000 as a mortgage. No one lost. The bank was satisfied that it had made a good business deal, and the congregation still owned the property. The children of light had learned from the children of darkness—or was it the other way around?

[376] In past generations craftsmen were proud of making things that would last a lifetime. Today mass production has eroded that pride of workmanship, and most manufactured items have built-in obsolescence. Autos and appliances are made to wear out so that we will have to purchase replacements and thus keep the factories humming. In this situation, ethics and economics come into serious conflict, and idealism is the victim. Everyone who does a useful job on an assembly line, on a farm, in a garage, in a hospital, or in a church needs to be able to take pride in the product of his efforts.

[377] The Priceless Ingredient of every product in the marketplace is the honor and integrity of him who makes it.
HAKEEN, *the wise philosopher of Baghdad*

[378] The Duke of Florence came upon a young workman on his estate who was fitting together a box with infinite care and patience. "To what use is that box to be put?" the duke asked.

"Flowers will be planted in it, sir," the young man answered.

"Then it will be filled with dirt! Why take such pains to make each joint and surface perfect?" persisted the duke.

"I love perfect things," the workman answered.

"It's wasted effort," said the duke. "No one will observe its perfection."

"My spirit will," said the young man. "Do you suppose the Carpenter of Nazareth ever made anything less well than he could? Was he satisfied with anything less than perfect?"

"That's sacrilege and impudence," stormed the duke. "What's your name?"

"Michelangelo Buonarroti, sir," the young man answered.

No wonder Michelangelo's work still inspires people after five centuries!

[379] Souls are built as temples are:
Here a carving rich and quaint,
There the image of a saint,
Here a deep-toned pane to tell
Sacred truth or miracle.
Every little helps the much;
Every cheerful, careless touch
Adds a charm or leaves a scar.
Souls are built as temples are.
Build it well, whate'er you do!
Build it straight and strong and true.
Build it clear and high and broad.
Build it for the eye of God!

INTRODUCTIONS AND INVOCATIONS

[380] Prayers that open public gatherings are rather perfunctory, but once in a while one of them shakes up the troops. As the Colorado State Senate began its session one day, its chaplain prayed, "We thank thee, O God, this morning that we are alive, sober, and not in jail." And one humorist commented about the chaplain of the United States Senate that "he looks over the senators and then prays for the country."

[381] A speaker wanted to establish a folksy and intimate relationship with his audience, so he began: "I address you tonight as my friends. Because I know you so well, I will not call you 'Ladies and Gentlemen.' "

[382] For an after-dinner program:
Every rose has its thorn
And fuzz grows on peaches.
You've had your dinner
So now listen to speeches.

[383] Norman Thomas once said there are three kinds of chairmen (or chairpersons, to update the term) at public meetings: chairmen who desire to prove that they can make a better speech than the speaker and try to do it; chairmen who fear the speaker is about to administer ideological poison to an innocent audience and try to give an antidote in advance; and chairmen who believe it is their duty to practice reading a speaker's obituary.

[384] Mark Twain and Chauncey M. Depew, both gifted after-dinner speakers, once found themselves sharing the same program. Twain spoke first and received a great ovation. When Depew was introduced, he said, "This audience ought to know that before the dinner started, Twain and I exchanged speeches. He gave my speech, but unfortunately I've lost his."

After the dinner an Englishman came up to Twain and said, "You were imposed upon. That speech was pure rot."

[385] If people straggle in late, they may be like little Johnny. Johnny was loitering and watching a baseball game when an older friend noticed him and said, "Johnny, you'd better hurry home or you'll be late for dinner." But Johnny said, "No, I won't be late. I've got the meat."

LABOR

[386] Hard work is beneficial, much as we hate to admit it. John Buchan in *Memory Hold-the-Door* imagines a future without work and finds it a nightmare. Science has won all its major victories, there's abundance for all, and no need for anyone to put out effort. The world has become a smooth-running machine. But there's also no need to think, so everyone becomes "slightly idiotic." And life is spent only for amusement, so that "behind the mask of riotous living there is death at the heart."

[387] Two men worked together for years, and finally one of them was made foreman of the crew. He immediately went to his friend and told him, "You're fired."

"Why?" asked the other fellow in astonishment.

"Just to show you who's boss, that's why," said the new foreman.

[388] Work is the inevitable condition of human life, the true source of human welfare.
TOLSTOI

LAW AND JUSTICE

[389] In a discussion about keeping the Ten Commandments, a man commented, "I've done pretty well. I think I deserve a passing grade." That sounds fine, but what is a passing grade? In school, it is about 70 percent. Does that mean that if we keep seven out of the Ten Commandments, we pass? I doubt it. Most people who are in jail have obeyed 70 percent of the laws. It's the one law they broke that got them into trouble.

[390] I believe you are guilty and would wish to condemn you severely, but through a petty technicality I am obliged to discharge you. I know you are guilty and so do you. I wish you to remember that you will some day pass before a better and wiser judge, where you will be dealt with according to justice and not according to man's law.
JUSTICE HORACE GRAY

[391] There is in human nature a disposition to evil, and that government is not government which cannot restrain it; and that religion is satanic which does not seek incessantly to overcome it.
WALTER LIPPMAN

[392] Fortunately this is a dependable world. Laws of nature work for our good when we cooperate with them. The force of gravity, for instance, will bring a person crashing to death if that person jumps from the top of a tall building. But the same law of gravity makes it possible for us to walk on the ground or to build a house without the fear that it will float off into the sky. It is therefore better for us to work with nature's laws rather than to ask God to perform miracles that countermand them.

LOVE

[393] During World War I in France a nightingale had its nest in a tree near the trenches. In the silence between volleys, its song could be heard. The thunder of the guns would drown it out, but when they fell silent, its glad notes were flung out above the battlefield. It was singing a love song to its mate, and even in that timid bird love could cast out fear.

[394] Love cures people—both the ones who give it and the ones who receive it.
KARL MENNINGER

[395] Because we are loved, we are able to love. Because grace is given to us, we are able to be gracious to others. On the Irish coast there are twin lighthouses, set about 500 feet apart on opposite sides of an estuary. There is a powerful light in one, but no light in the other, only prisms and reflectors that mirror the light from the first. Yet from a distance, both seem to shine equally. Just so our lives can reflect and mirror the love and grace of God.

LOYALTY

[396] At the close of the Civil War General Robert E. Lee had won the admiration of both the North and the South. He was offered high-paying jobs, but typically chose to follow a path of honesty and duty. "I am grateful," he said, "but I cannot desert my native state in the hour of her adversity. I must abide her fortunes and share her fate." Lee therefore accepted the position of president of Washington College (now Washington and Lee University) at Lexington, Virginia.

[397] Our college football team used to "die for dear old Wagner" every Saturday afternoon. It was a bad season, and when the final game pitted us against a much stronger opponent the newspapers suggested that the score would be 50-0. But before the game the coach, who had scolded and cajoled the players all year long, took a different approach. "You men can forget this season, and you'll

have a fresh start next year," he said. "As for me, I'll lose my job, my reputation, and my honor. It all depends on how you play today." So, with the coach's words fresh on their minds, the team went out to play a strong opponent. Would they let him down? It would be nice to report that they won, but they didn't. However, the final score was 7-6, and it seemed like a victory. Why the change? It was a response to an appeal by the coach for personal loyalty. Such loyalty to our ideals, to institutions, or to a leader can encourage us to do our best.

[398] During the battle of Yorktown, which ended the Revolutionary War, the Americans needed to dislodge the enemy troops from a large house they used as headquarters. The building happened to be the home of Thomas Nelson, former governor of Virgina, who was commanding the American artillery. Knowing what it meant, Nelson commanded, "Sergeant, train your cannon on my home." The guns roared and the cannonballs found their mark, bringing the victory closer. Nelson's patriotism enabled him to contribute his most cherished possession—his home—to the cause of American freedom. Millions of others have given up their homes for similar causes that they regarded as just and necessary, by leaving them to go into military service or sometimes by seeing them destroyed by bombs and fire.

[399] Napoleon is said to have commanded intense loyalty from his troops. A preacher of the era asked one soldier, "Did you men like Napoleon?"

The veteran replied, "Like him? We believe in him. If Napoleon said, 'Go to the moon' every man would start. Napoleon would find the way!"

[400] According to a legend, when Jesus ascended to heaven, he was met by the angel Gabriel. "What have you achieved?" asked Gabriel.

"I have left behind 11 men who believe in me," said Jesus.

"Is that all?" demanded the angel.

"That is all," Jesus replied.

"But what if they fail?" Gabriel persisted.

Confidently, Jesus replied, "I know them, and they will not fail."

[401] Too many people take seriously the advice of Charles Dickens' character Mr. Pickwick. Asked what he would do if caught in a political demonstration, Pickwick said, "Shout with the crowd." But suppose there were two crowds on opposing sides, he was asked. "I'd shout with the loudest," he said.

MARRIAGE AND FAMILY

[402] An ancient marriage custom in the Druse tribe of Syria requires the bride to present her husband with a handsome dagger to use on her if she proves unfaithful.

[403] One of King Solomon's great weaknesses was his affinity for idolatrous women. He is reported to have had 700 wives and 300 concubines. Maybe that is gross exaggeration—maybe it only seemed like 1000. Nevertheless, it was a great crime against women and against morality, particularly since he permitted them to bring their idols into Jerusalem and to worship strange gods. Despite the vaunted glory of Solomon's kingdom, five years after his death the nation was torn apart and Jerusalem was plundered.

[404] Commenting on the failure of parents to teach religion to their children, Harry Emerson Fosdick said, "I believe that 75 percent of all parents are liabilities."

"Oh, that figure must be wrong," someone protested.

"Yes," answered Fosdick, "I guess I should have said 85 percent."

[405] "How's your wife?" an absentminded clergyman asked.

"Why, my wife died and went to heaven," the man answered.

"I'm sorry," the clergyman started to say, but that didn't sound right. "I'm glad," he then started to say, but that too sounded improper. So he wound up saying, "I'm surprised!"

[406] The parents of a 10-year-old girl were naturally concerned when their daughter went off to summer camp for the first time.

Trying to cheer them up, she sent her first letter home a few days later. "Dear Mom and Dad: Your worries are over. I am really growing up. I'm in a tent with older girls, and all we talk about is boys and sex. Please send me a water pistol. Love, Linda."

[407] The late Dr. Franklin Clark Fry enjoyed telling a story about women who were overly suspicious of their husbands. When Adam stayed out very late for a few nights, Eve became upset. "You're running around with other women," she charged.

"You're being unreasonable," Adam responded. "You're the only woman on earth."

The quarrel continued until Adam fell asleep, only to be awakened by someone poking him in the chest. It was Eve.

"What do you think you're doing?" Adam demanded.

"Counting your ribs," said Eve.

[408] The archbishop preached on the beauties of married life, and after the mass two women stood outside the cathedral, surrounded by their flock of children. "That was a fine sermon on marriage that his Reverence gave us," one woman said.

"Indeed it was," responded the other. "And I just wish I knew as little about the matter as he does!"

[409] Socrates was once asked whether it is better for a man to marry or to remain single. "No matter which, he'll repent of it," the philosopher replied.

[410] An American tourist was shocked to see a man riding on his burro while the man's wife walked along behind them. "Why doesn't your wife ride on a burro?" the tourist demanded.

The man replied simply, "My wife doesn't own a burro."

[411] Home is heaven for beginners.
CHARLES H. PARKHURST

[412] Variety is important in life, and when things go too smoothly they may need to be stirred up. On a pastoral visit, Dr. Thomas

Chalmers of Scotland called on a shoemaker and his wife. Seeking to impress the minister with their piety, they recounted their blessings. "Yes," said the shoemaker, "my wife and I have lived together for these 30 years without a single quarrel."

That was too much for the feisty clergyman. He thumped his cane on the floor and said, "Terribly monotonous, man. Terribly monotonous."

[413] At their golden wedding a couple was asked for the secret of their happy marriage. "We found quite a few things we could agree on," they said. In keeping with this theme, a premarital clinic for engaged couples asked the couples to mark on a printed sheet their attitudes toward many fundamental things—religion, family, work, children. Then the two sheets were put together and held up to the light. If their attitudes agreed and the marks coincided, they were deemed suited for each other. If too many of the marks were different, there was danger ahead.

[414] A cartoon in the *New Yorker* showed a father scowling over a very bad report card while his little boy stood by, asking, "What do you think it is, Dad? Heredity or environment?"

[415] Adam and Eve didn't have a marriage license or a wedding ring or a bridal trousseau. As a matter of fact, they didn't have any clothes or a clergyman or a wedding service. Yet God sanctified their marriage. Diamond rings and marriage certificates and bridal garments and elaborate church rituals are only symbols. True marriage is the perfect fusion of two lives so that neither is complete without the other.

[416] Two little girls were playing together and one said, "When I grow up, I'm going to marry Cousin Ellen."

The other responded wisely, "You can't do that. She's a lady. You have to marry a man."

The first girl protested, "Why do I have to marry a man?"

Said her friend, "It's like this: if two men got married, their children would have two papas and no mama."

MERCY

[417] When we pray, "Lord, be merciful to me, a sinner," does it really help? Maybe the answer lies in an incident that took place in 1347, when King Edward III of England invaded France and besieged the city of Calais. Because of the city's resistance, he promised to destroy it. Finally the city's burgesses came out and pleaded for clemency if they surrendered. The king answered, "My word is pledged. I cannot go back."

But then Queen Philippa interposed, saying, "I pray thee, gentle sir, for love of me, forgive them." And the city was saved.

[418] The difference between justice and mercy is dramatically shown in an incident—probably apocryphal—attributed to Napoleon.

A young soldier had been found guilty of sleeping while on sentry duty and had been sentenced to death. His distraught mother finally got an interview with Napoleon to plead for her son. He was her only child; he was young; he had an otherwise blameless record.

"Yet he endangered the entire army by his action," said Napoleon. "Justice demands that he should die."

"True, sire," responded the woman. "But I plead not for justice, but for mercy."

"Very well then," answered Napoleon, "I will have mercy."

[419] The quality of mercy is not strained,
It droppeth as the gentle dew from heaven
Upon the place beneath: it is twice blessed;
It blesseth him that gives and him that takes:
'Tis mightiest in the mightiest; it becomes
The throned monarch better than his crown.
SHAKESPEARE

[420] Coventry Patmore's poem "The Toys" tells of a disobedient child who was sent to bed as punishment. Later his father, relenting, crept into the youngest's room. He found the child asleep, his face still wet with tears. Near his bed, on a table, he had gathered his favorite toys—marbles, shells, coins—to comfort his sad small

heart. As the father kissed away the lad's tears, he realized that God must feel toward his children just as he felt toward his own sleeping child.

> And thou rememberest of what toys
> We made our joys,
> How weakly understood
> Thy great commanded good,
> Then fatherly not less
> Than I whom Thou hast moulded from the clay,
> Thou'lt leave Thy wrath, and say,
> "I will be sorry for their childishness."

MISSIONS

[421] An American plane was wrecked in a South Seas jungle during World War II. To seek aid for a wounded crew member, the pilot made his way toward a native village. He was unsure whether or not the natives would be friendly, but because his companion needed help he walked boldly into it. Burly natives seized him, tied him up, and took him to their chief. The pilot feared for his life. but the chief addressed him in surprisingly good English: "You American?" Then the chief told the warriors to untie him, adding, "You have nothing to fear, American. Your missionaries have brought Christ here."

[422] Can you convey the image of God to others? This is often called evangelism or witnessing, and you do it when you do good to others or when you share something with others in God's name. A missionary doctor in a field hospital treated a sick man who began to improve and recover. One day the doctor stopped at the man's bedside and in the course of conversation asked, "Do you believe in God and in Jesus Christ?"

The man replied, "Oh, yes, doctor. I believe in God and Jesus Christ—and, doctor, I believe in you." The kindness and help he had received seemed to represent God.

[423] When Florence Nightingale ministered to a stricken soldier in the Crimean War, he looked up at her and said, "You look like the grace of God."

[424] Life began at 47 for "Father" Heyer—Carl Friedrich Heyer, a Lutheran minister. After years of missionary work on the American frontier in the Mississippi and Ohio Valleys, Heyer in 1840 at the age of 47 learned of India with its millions of superstitious and underprivileged people. Once in India, he saw the great need for health care, so at 53 he came back to the United States for medical training. After 17 years of productive service in India, Heyer "retired" at 64 and became a traveling preacher in Minnesota, going from settlement to settlement in his wagon, preaching and baptizing. In 1868, when he was 75, he heard that missionary work in India was being dropped. He pleaded with a Lutheran convention in Pittsburgh to continue support for missions in India, but others argued that no missionary could be sent because of the shortages of money and manpower following the Civil War. Dramatically, Heyer marched up to the platform and held up his carpet bag, saying, "Here I am. Send me!" The group responded to his gesture, so at 77 Heyer went back to Rajahmundry and worked like a young man, holding the mission program together until younger men could come and relieve him.

[425] Someone asked the Duke of Wellington if he believed in foreign missions. He answered, "I am a soldier. Christ is my commanding officer and yours. What are his orders?"

"Go into all the world and preach the gospel to every creature," was the response.

"Enough!" exclaimed the Iron Duke. "There is no question. Those are orders."

[426] Fritz Kreisler once coveted a beautiful Guarnerius violin. He heard its lovely tone and offered all he possessed for it but found it had already been sold to a collector. "That divine voice doomed to silence under a glass case in a collector's museum was a tragedy that rent my heart," Kreisler wrote. The violinist kept on the trail of the owner, pleading and threatening.

Finally the collector took the violin out of its locked case, handed it to Kreisler, and said, "Play." Kreisler tuned up the instrument and played as if his life depended on it. Moved by the performance, the collector said, "I have no right to it. Keep it. Take it out into the world and let it be heard."

Isn't that what we're told to do with the good news of God's love? Take it out into the world and let it be heard!

[427] Early Lutheran missionaries in the West Indies served the Danish landlords who ruled the islands, now the United States territory of the Virgin Islands. One of the pastors asked, "What of the Negro slaves in the fields? Who ministers to them?"

He was discourteously told, "If you want to preach to them, go out into the fields where they work. We don't want them in our church."

The pastor did so, and today large Lutheran congregations in the Virgin Islands testify to the pioneer preacher who went into the fields and into the slaves' quarters to preach the freedom that Christ brought.

MODERN LIFE

[428] A young businesswoman was approached by a real estate agent who wanted to sell her a home. "A home?" she said. "Why do I need a home? I was born in a hospital, educated in a boarding school, courted in an automobile, married in a church. We eat in restaurants, spend our mornings playing golf and our afternoons playing bridge at the club. Evenings we go to the movies, and when I die I'm going to be buried from a funeral home. I don't need a home. All I need is a garage!"

[429] Life is often too agitated, hectic and frantic. Kenneth Fearing's "Dirge" points this out:

> "And wow he died as wow he lived,
> Going whop to the office and blooie home to sleep and biff got married
> and bam he had children and oof he got fired,
> Zowie did he live and zowie did he die. . . ."

[430] The most effective warning to young people against drugs or promiscuity is to awaken them to the value of life. As God's children, we are priceless. A store was holding a clothing sale and

placed in its window a large sign, "Slightly soiled—Greatly reduced in price." So are many lives—slightly soiled but terribly cheapened. How much are you worth—in God's sight and in your own?

[431] Architecture has been revolutionized by electricity. Theaters, schools, factories, office buildings, and even dwellings are built without windows. The interior is air-conditioned and dark, lighted only by human means. Unfortunately, life itself for many people has become like that, too. They deliberately shut out the light and live in artificial gloom, eternal spiritual darkness. They forget that Jesus said, "I am the light of the world."

[432] A wealthy Chicago man engaged some world-famous doctors to attend his sick daughter. The event attracted media atttention and reporters went to the man's house to get the story. They were met by a servant and their first question was about the nature of the girl's illness. "I don't know exactly what the trouble is," she said, "but it must be terrible because it costs so much to cure it."

[433] Before the *Titanic* struck an iceberg and went down to a watery grave on its maiden trans-Atlantic voyage, the ship had for 15 hours been receiving radio warnings about the danger of icebergs in its path. Meanwhile the passengers pursued their full program of hilarity, drinking, and dancing, while powerful engines pushed the ship ahead at full speed. Channing Pollock wrote later, "This is the staggering fact about our contemporary world—engines at full speed, bands playing, passengers dancing, and nobody caring a damn."

[434] There's something to be said for the concept of the quiet Puritan Sunday, a day of absolute and enforced rest. The wheels of industry came to a halt; the family stayed home or in its neighborhood; there were supposed to be no "worldly" distractions from worship. Maybe this was too strict, but most of our modern plague of stomach ulcers, stress, and breakdowns could be avoided if we recognized the importance of rest and quiet. From a purely physical standpoint, the idea of a day each week for change, rest, and quiet relaxation is beneficial. This may seem to have nothing to do with

religion, but remember that God knows what's good for us physically, too.

[435] Ring Lardner is above all the historian of frustration; of courtships that go on the rocks or, what is worse, end in marriage; of honeymoons that fizzle out; of marriages that turn sour; of plays that flop, prizefights that are fixed, games that blow up, beauty that is skin deep, affection that is phony, talent that is meretricious. Thus his account of "How to write short stories" closes with the recommendations that ambitious writers "take up the life of a mule in the Grand Canyon. The mule watches the trains come in from the East, he watches the trains come in from the West, and keeps wondering who is going to ride him. But he never finds out." The mule is the symbol for all Lardner's characters; they wait, and nothing happens, nor do they ever find out.
HENRY STEELE COMMAGER

MORALITY

[436] Recently the United States Department of State cracked down on some American companies that did business abroad, fining them great sums because they had bribed officials in several countries. The companies were shocked and perplexed, because without making such payments they would not be able to operate in those foreign lands. The officials in the foreign lands were equally upset, because such payments for the privilege of doing business were a normal expense in their lands. The problem arises whenever we try to impose our standards of morality on others, especially when we believe that we have a higher or better standard. The best way to preserve morality, whether it be in our neighborhood or in the world, is by a good example.

[437] In ancient times sea water was poured into large, shallow pans. The sun dried up the water and left a residue of salt, highly prized for cooking and as a preservative. However, the salt had to be used quickly or it gathered odors and lost its saltiness. Once spoiled, it had to be thrown out. Now salt is produced commercially and carefully treated by the addition of sodium carbonate or some

similar chemical which has the effect of wrapping each grain of salt in a protective covering. The flavor is thus locked in, and moisture is kept out. If we are indeed the "salt of the earth," our lives can remain pure and useful only when they are wrapped in the protective power and Spirit of God.

[438] Our generation is probably no worse than any other. Colonial America was wide open and immoral in many ways. The frontiers of the Wild West were noted for their moral laxity. There were times when state legislatures had to adjourn because most of the members were drunk. Until the awakening of a social conscience early in the 19th century, human slavery was not only condoned but promoted. The Victorian period clamped a corset of piety around people, but the vices did not go away; they simply went under cover. Today's moral freedom offers a wholesome challenge because it overlooks divorce and drinking and sexual deviations, thereby putting it squarely up to each of us to act decently and in accordance with divine law.

MOTHERS

[439] In 1906 the steamship *General Slocum* sank in New York Harbor while carrying about 1500 passengers on a Sunday school outing. It was one of the great marine disasters, and it nearly wiped out a New York City church. Among the few picked up from the water and rescued was a boy who said, "My mother gave me a life preserver, and that's how I got saved. I guess she didn't have any for herself, because they can't find her."

[440] A teacher in a nursery class asked the children, "Who is always with us to help us be good?" Then she explained that the answer was "God."

One youngster piped up, "Well, maybe it's God, but mothers help a lot."

[441] A mother had three children. In the morning, each child came and said, "Mother, I love you." She then asked each one to do some little chore. The first refused and went away. The second

promised gladly and then forgot. The third child immediately did as he was bidden. Which one of these three really loved the mother?

[442] There was nothing glamorous about Tillie Maczek of Chicago, but she deserved to be honored as a great mother. In 1944 she put an ad in a Chicago newspaper, "$5000 reward for information leading to the arrest of the killers of Officer Lundy in 1932." Investigation revealed that her son Joe had been sentenced to life imprisonment for the alleged murder, although he had insisted on his innocence. No one believed him but his mother, but what could she do? She was an ignorant Polish immigrant, scarcely able to speak English, and her husband was a stockyard worker who had died shortly after their marriage. So Tillie scrubbed floors in Chicago office buildings for years, relentlessly toiling for her child. Finally she had saved up $5000 from her meager pay and put the ad in the paper. Of course, it attracted attention. The newspaper itself became interested in the case and took up her cause. Joe was eventually found innocent and released from prison. A mother's faith and devotion had brought about a happy ending—as it so often does!

[443] A cartoon showed a child stumbling over a stone and saying, "Mommy, why don't you look where I'm going?"

NATION

[444] When the Constitutional Convention met in 1787, Benjamin Franklin moved to open the sessions with prayer. "I have lived a long time, and the longer I live the more convincing proofs I see that God governs the affairs of men," he said. "We have been assured in the sacred writings that 'except the Lord build the house, they labor in vain that build it.' I firmly believe this and I also believe that without God's aid, we shall not succeed in our political building."

[445] The religious foundation for American life was expressed by George Washington when he said, "It is my earnest prayer to God

that he would be most graciously pleased to dispose us to do justice, to love mercy, and to demean ourselves with charity, humility, and the pacific temper of mind which were the characteristics of the Divine Author of our religion, without a humble imitation of whose example in these things we cannot hope to be a happy nation."

[446] The American way of life honors God as man's creator, recognizes those who trust in him as brethren, and counts the life of every man, woman, and child to be of infinite value. This faith of our fathers must be made available to all mankind now and for generations to come.
ADMIRAL CHESTER W. NIMITZ

OPPORTUNITY

[447] The motto of Spain in 1490 was *"Ne plus ultra,"* meaning "No more beyond." Spain was then a great empire, ruling parts of Europe, Africa, and the Atlantic isles. Three years later the report of Columbus changed all that, perhaps to *"Plus ultra."* There was much more beyond the sea than ever they had imagined. But hasn't it always been so? Alexander the Great is said to have wept because there were no more worlds to conquer! And every once in a while we hear that the frontiers are gone and we must despair because nothing good lies ahead. But the prophets of doom have always been wrong. Opportunities for growth within ourselves, beyond ourselves, and toward better relations between us are greater than ever before.

[448] The builders of the Panama Canal had a poetic slogan:

Got any river they say isn't crossable?
Got any mountains that can't be cut through?
We specialize in the wholly impossible,
Doing things nobody ever could do.

[449] When oil was discovered in Oklahoma, a reporter was sent from an Eastern newspaper to write a story on the changes it made in the life of the people. He found one elderly couple who had

moved from North Carolina to Oklahoma, taken some land, and for years scraped out a hard living farming it. Then one day a man took a sample of their water and offered to buy the farm. In a short time the most productive oil well in the area was situated between the house and the barn. The old farmer said, "To think that we slaved here for years, and all the time this was right under our doorstep and we never knew it."

[450] The greatest moment of a person's life is when he turns the corner of a street and meets a new thought, impulse, or idea.
RALPH WALDO EMERSON

[451] It's easy to say we would do something great "if I had the money . . . if I were in his shoes . . . if I had the time . . . if I were younger." The secret of success lies in using the resources at hand. For example, look at Shamgar—even if you have never before heard of him. All we know about Shamgar is in one line from the book of Judges, in the Old Testament: "After him was Shamgar the son of Anath, who killed six hundred of the Philistines with an oxgoad" (Judges 3:31). Evidently Shamgar was a farmer who had only an oxgoad for a weapon but who led a foray against the strong and powerful Philistine army. He was no military genius, and his weapon was surely inferior to those of the enemy. But he saw the need to drive a marauding opponent from his land, and he responded with determination. With God's help the oxgoad was mightier than the army of the Philistines.

[452] A man watched great logs being loaded on a ship. He pictured their many uses—strong beams to support a lofty church tower or a fine home, tall masts for some sailing ship, poles to be used to display a high-flying flag. Then he discovered that instead of this, the logs were intended for a match factory, where they would be cut into tiny matchsticks. At first he felt indignant about this debasement of tall trees, but then he reflected on the utility of matches. A match can light a fire to warm a home; it can light a candle whose tiny flame can conquer darkness. Even the little things, the humble things, are needed for effective living.

[453] Don't give up too soon! During World War I, the British and Austrian armies were locked in a bitter battle near Vienna on March 19, 1917. Both sides suffered great losses with no territory gained. The British leaders came to the conclusion that it was hopeless to continue, so under cover of darkness they withdrew their forces to regroup elsewhere. On the other side of the barbed wire, the Austrians were doing the same. When the light of dawn came, the field of battle was deserted. Either side could have taken it bloodlessly if it had only stuck it out.

[454] Some years ago a large cruise ship went aground on a coral reef off Bermuda. The engines strained to pull it free, but finally the passengers had to be sent ashore in small boats. When the time of month came for the moon's gravitational pull to produce an exceptionally high tide, tugboats surrounded the vessel, and at the flood of the tide they all pulled and tugged while the ship churned the sea with its propeller. For a time nothing happened, but dramatically, just at the crest of the tide, the big ship moved a few inches, then a few feet, and finally free from the sand that had held it. As the poet said, there are tides in the affairs of men, tides of the spirit. They come upon us unexpectedly, for they cannot be predicted like ocean tides. "God comes without bell," an old writer said. We need to be watchful and ready when these spiritual opportunities come.

[455] General Ulysses S. Grant was badly beaten in the battle of Shiloh, Tennessee. His aide, General James McPherson, reported the loss of half of the Union artillery and almost one-third of the troops during the bloody conflict. Logic called for a retreat, but Grant ordered, "Reform the lines and we will attack at dawn. We will take them by surprise." By nine o'clock the next morning the South's troops were being routed by the surprise attack from the weary Union troops. The confederates had felt so secure in their previous day's victory that they forgot to be alert.

[456] Joan of Arc told King Charles of France of the heavenly voices which called her to lead the armies of France. The king

was petulant. "Voices, voices! Why don't they come to me? I am the king, not you."

Joan answered, "They do come to you, but you don't hear them. When the angelus rings, you cross yourself and are done with it; but if you prayed from your heart and listened, you would hear as I do."

[457] A newspaper account told of a farmer in South Africa who had worked the same fields for 30 years. He barely eked out a living on his small farm. Because the soil was getting poorer, he plowed a little deeper one year. Below the soil which he had worked for so long he found a stratum of gold-bearing quartz. In one plowing he got more reward than for 30 years of toil—because he plowed a little deeper.

[458] The day is short, the work is great, the reward is rich, and the Master is urgent.

TALMUD

[459] Do things really work together for good? Like an oyster, can we take the hurting, annoying intrusion of an irritating grain of evil and put a lovely iridescent coating around it to make it a pearl? Great souls have done this throughout the years, converting incipient tragedy into triumph. In one section of Alabama, the boll weevil ruined cotton crops and brought starvation and deprivation to the farmers. As a result they were forced to change their one-crop system and diversify. Now in the town of Enterprise there stands a monument to the boll weevil, bearing the inscription: "In profound appreciation of the boll weevil and what it has done as a herald of prosperity, this tablet is erected by the citizens of Enterprise."

PATIENCE

[460] "Be prepared" is more than a Boy Scout motto. Many times a whole life is spent in preparation. A musician may study for 20 years or more before giving a first solo recital. A physician spends

20 years in school and college plus several years of internship before plunging into private practice.

Once when Daniel Webster finished a thrilling oration in the U.S. Senate, a friend rushed up to congratulate him and gushed, "The best part of your speech was that it was so completely extemporaneous."

Webster growled in reply, "Nonsense! I've been getting ready to make that speech for 40 years."

A similar answer was given by an elderly clergyman when a well-wisher said, "That was a wonderful sermon. How long did it take you to prepare it?"

The minister answered, "All my life."

[461] Calmness, self-possession, and silence are often the best answers to insults or unfair accusations. When Washington was accused of drunkenness, immorality, treason, and a desire to be king, he refused to reply. Lincoln, slandered and vilified for his war policies, met all with dignified silence.

In a little North Carolina town many years ago a Methodist minister enraged some of his parishioners by befriending and helping black people. One former army colonel took particular offense and when he saw the minister on the street, he greeted him with a loud outburst of abuse and blistering profanity. The minister stood still, white-faced but calm, while the tirade continued. Finally the angry abuse stopped and the minister said, "Is that all? Then I bid you good morning." He quietly stepped around the still-enraged but now deflated colonel and went his way.

[462] When Daniel Webster was a young lawyer he took a case for a fee of $20. It was a difficult case and in preparing for it he had to make a trip to Boston, which in itself cost more than he was getting as a fee. He was determined to do a thorough job on the case and win it, which he did. Many years later a big company wanted him at short notice to undertake a case for what was in those days a fabulous fee. Webster looked over the case and found it was almost identical with the one he had researched and won 20 years before! His faithfulness was rewarded, even if it took 20 years.

[463] The immense nation of China has been invaded dozens of times in its 6000 years of history. Under many dynasties the Chinese people had brilliant technology and culture, but they were never warlike. China has never won a war. Yet Chinese life has gone on unaffected, and invaders were eventually assimilated into the Chinese culture. By yielding and enveloping, China gained the final triumph even when the invaders "won the war."

PEACE

[464] If we are to have a decent peace and a decent world after the peace, two things must happen. Religion must expand and take in a lot more territory, and we must have a tremendous revival of the missionary crusade. It doesn't make much difference what else we do, unless we do this.
VICE-PRESIDENT HENRY WALLACE

[465] An old legend says that the robe which Jesus wore before his crucifixion and for which the soldiers around the cross cast lots had magical powers. Its particular virtue was that it brought peace to its owner. Lloyd Douglas wove his novel *The Robe* around this legend. Like all legends, it has a grain of truth behind it. In a deeper sense, what the Bible calls the "robe of righteousness" or the "garments of salvation" actually do bring peace to people who wrap themselves in them.

[466] Be at peace with yourself first and then you will be able to bring peace to others.
THOMAS À. KEMPIS

[467] A little boy was asked to recite Psalm 23. Either he did not know it at all or he knew it very well. He said, "The Lord is my shepherd. I should worry!"

[468] Some years ago a rather elaborate home was built in my neighborhood. One of its features was a concrete-lined subcellar, to be used for food storage and as a bomb shelter in case of nuclear attack. This notion that such shelters could offer protection was exploited

at the time. One newspaper ad read, "What if atomic bombs fall? Buy one of our 10-acre desert tracts in Arizona. Full price $250." Considering inflation, that may have been a good investment, but it really was a ridiculous concept of the way to find peace and safety.

[469] In 1902 a serious boundary dispute threatened war between Argentina and Chile. The Roman Catholic archbishop of Argentina opposed the military preparations, saying it was wrong for a Christian land to fight against its brothers. The bishop of Chile agreed, and together they influenced their governments to call in the mediation of King Edward of England to settle the dispute. An amicable agreement was reached, and at the new boundary line a huge statue, the *Christ of the Andes,* was erected. Its inscription reads, "Sooner shall these mountains crumble into dust than Argentina and Chile violate the pledge of peace and love they have made at the feet of Christ their Savior."

POWER

[470] Men are four:
He who knows and knows not that he knows. He is asleep; wake
 him.
He who knows not and knows not that he knows not. He is a fool;
 shun him.
He who knows not and knows that he knows not. He is a child;
 teach him.
He who knows and knows that he knows. He is a king; follow him.
Chinese proverb

[471] Some day people will learn that material things do not bring happiness and are of little use in making men and women creative and powerful. Then the scientists of the world will turn their laboratories over to the study of God and prayer and spiritual forces that have as yet been hardly guessed at. When that day comes, the world will see more progress in one generation than it has seen in the past four.
CHARLES P. STEINMETZ

[472] The quest for power is usually based on the good that a person claims he will do with it, however fraudulent that claim may be. Hitler said he sought nothing personal, only the good of his nation. Stalin claimed that he was protecting the rights of the common people. Even in our limited sphere, we think that if we were elected president, what great good things we would do for the country; or if we had a million dollars, what good we would do with it. Unfortunately, however, power corrupts almost everyone. We are thankful for the few exceptions, like George Washington, who refused a third term as president lest too much power be centralized in the presidency.

[473] Government officials insist that we need to spend hundreds of billions of dollars for military superiority in order to insure peace. However, the security of power is a delusion. People who are "on top of the world" can easily slip off. Alexander the Great is a perfect example. His father was Philip of Macedon, a wise and crafty king who built up the world's most powerful army. He turned his realm over to Alexander with the advice that he conquer every other force that might challenge his rule. According to Philip's reasoning, this would assure peace and prosperity throughout the known world. Alexander followed his father's advice. His force swept through Asia and Africa, defeating every other nation and gaining control of vast territories. Alexander started his conquests at age 18 and never lost a battle. According to tradition, he wept when there were no more worlds to conquer, no more battles to fight. He had won everything—but he died at age 32 in a strange land, hated by many of his soldiers. Within a generation the empire fell apart.

[474] A few years ago on Long Island I went through a giant new power plant. The gleaming turbine was five stories high, and there were giant towers, all silent and tomblike, because they were not yet operating. Outside the building was noisy chugging and clatter. It turned out to be a small gasoline engine busily pumping water out into the harbor. It seemed a sort of parable. The big plant had all the equipment but no power. The little engine was chugging away and accomplishing a lot more.

In the Bible, Paul warns Timothy about people like that, who hold to "the form of religion but [deny] the power of it" (2 Tim. 3:5).

PRAYER

[475] Prayer may change *things;* but, much more important, it changes *us.*

[476] Some people save their prayers for Sunday, as if they were making a long-distance call when the rates are lower. Prayer is a free call, an 800 number, a direct line to God open every minute of the day.

[477] In all ages people have said, "Show us God and then we will pray." That's why the heathen made idols of gold or brass and why the ancient Greeks personified their gods. Oddly enough, the Christian faith demands an exactly opposite attitude. It says, "Pray—and then you will see God."

[478] During the New York World's Fair, its director, Grover Whelan, refused to be bothered by visitors. One morning a young man hustled right past the receptionist's desk and started into Whelan's office. "Sorry, you can't go in there," the receptionist protested. "Mr. Whelan won't talk with anyone now."

"Listen," said the man. "I talk with God twice a day and he listens to me, so I guess I can talk to Grover Whelan."

[479] There is only one way to learn to write, I have often told students, and that way is to write, write, write. Write letters, stories, essays, memos, articles, descriptions, diaries. Practice makes perfect, and the more you write the easier writing becomes. But this is also true of prayer. The more you pray, the greater your ability to pray. People who say they can't pray either have not tried or are out of practice.

[480] God has three answers to prayer—yes, no, and wait. The first answer usually makes us joyful. The second answer makes most

people say their prayer was not answered. The third answer is hardest of all, because it makes us impatient and tests our faith, but it also gives us a chance to strengthen our hearts and hands to do God's will. A prayer answered before we are really ready can be dangerous.

[481] I discovered that after a time of prayer, I was able to do a far greater amount of work. A doctor has testified as a medical fact that my blood pressure was lowered by it, my nerves calmer, my mind rested and alert, my whole body in better health. I was refreshed and ready for work, and if previously I had been in a mood of pessimism and despair, after I prayed I was charged with new hope and confidence.
GANDHI

[482] From the diary of a soldier: "When you're lying in a foxhole wondering where the next bomb is going to drop, then you really start to pray. From the chaplain down to the lowest yardbird we were saying our prayers."

[483] An elderly lady was greatly troubled by the loss of a piece of jewelry and was advised to pray for help in finding it. At first she thought this was foolish and superstitious, but finally she agreed. As she prayed, she realized that she had hidden the jewelry in an old hatbox. Was it an answer to prayer? Or did her mental relaxation during the period of prayer help her to dredge up the answer from her subconscious? Either way, she found the jewelry.

[484] In the play *Father Malachy's Miracle* a quiet, gentle priest prays that a noisy and disturbing dance hall will move away from its site next to his church. His prayer is answered and the dance hall is transported to a rock in the ocean. This causes the priest no end of trouble, starting with the police, the lawyers, then the press, then the cardinals, and finally the pope himself. So the priest has to pray for a second miracle, to bring the dance hall back to its original location.

[485] Even if there were no god to hear and respond to prayer,

sincere prayer could change your life. Here are some things that praying does for you:

- it unifies your thoughts, making them coherent and consistent;
- it gives perspective, as climbing a tree when lost in the woods helps you get your bearings and find the right direction;
- it brings poise and peace, relieving anxiety, stimulating trust, easing a nagging conscience that makes us feel we must do something;
- it allows confession, the release of emotion and the pouring out of your deepest feelings as you would to an understanding friend or counselor;
- it corrects your motives ("We can pray for those we hate, but we can't hate those we pray for");
- it enriches personality by increasing your self-esteem;
- it gives power, reassurance, and improved morale.

[486] Some simple rules for prayer:

1. Have a regular time and place. Otherwise, prayer is easily crowded out of daily life.

2. Plan your prayer. Be specific. Maybe your requests have already been answered.

3. Prepare your heart. Try to feel the actual presence of God as you speak to him.

4. Relax your body. Be comfortable. Overcome tenseness and strain. Remember, God loves you exactly as you are.

5. Talk *with* God. Listen, learn, obey. Periods of silence give God a chance to speak, too.

6. Turn it over to God. After you've prayed, don't stew about it any longer. It's in good hands!

7. Pray always. If you pray only at church or in times of crisis, your prayers lose their relation to daily needs. In any situation it takes only a moment to shoot an arrow prayer toward God. "Lord, be merciful to me a sinner" was a prayer that won praise from Jesus. God is waiting, and when we are ready to pray, he is ready to hear and answer.

[487] Prayer is the hunger of the heart for God. When people are really hungry, food tastes especially good and they are more eager

137

for it. When ravenously hungry they sometimes say, "I'm so hungry I could eat nails." Without hunger the choicest food can seem flat and stale; with hunger the plainest fare tastes good. Prayer is the hunger that brings us to God so we may be filled with his blessings of inspiration, guidance, forgiveness, and comfort.

[488] During the bombing of London in World War II, a street sign said, "If your knees shake, kneel on them." During an earlier war, Abraham Lincoln expressed somewhat the same sentiment when he said, "I have often been driven to my knees by the realization that I have nowhere else to go."

[489] The early Egyptians depended on annual flooding of the Nile for their good crops. Receding flood waters left a rich black silt and assured the harvest. When the river failed to flood, it meant that the poor soil could produce very little, leading to a winter of hunger, so people thronged to their temples asking their gods to make the Nile overflow. Today the Aswan Dam controls the river's flow, and scientific planning sends the floods downriver at just the right time. In other places farmers often faced droughts that caused crop failure and poverty. All they could do about it was to pray for rain! But now vast irrigation systems have alleviated this condition. Does this mean that prayer is no longer necessary? Far from it! We've met some of our need for physical power, but our spiritual strength is actually weakened when we depend on mechanical resources rather than on God.

PREACHING

[490] Love and meekness become a preacher better than ambition. It is a good divine that follows his own instructions.
SHAKESPEARE

[491] A preacher's prayer:

Lord, fill my sermon with good stuff
And stop me when I've said enough. Amen.

[492] A good preacher should have these qualities and virtues:

First, he should be able to teach in a right and orderly way.
Second, he should have a good head.
Third, he should be able to speak well.
Fourth, he should have a good voice.
Fifth, a good memory.
Sixth, he should know when to stop.
Seventh, he should be sure of his material and diligent.
Eighth, he should stake body and life, goods and honor upon it.
Ninth, he must suffer himself to be vexed and flayed by everybody.
MARTIN LUTHER

[493] Sometimes a minister is called upon to say something, and sometimes he has something to say. Occasionally the two coincide.

[494] If I were to write of the burdens that a preacher must bear and endure, as I know them and myself experienced them, I would frighten everybody away from the ministry. For a devout, God-fearing preacher must be so minded that there is nothing he desires more than Christ, his Lord and Savior, and the eternal life to come, so that even though he lose his life and all else, Christ would still say to him, "Come unto me. You have been my beloved, faithful servant."
MARTIN LUTHER

[495] John Wanamaker, the Philadelphia merchant, was a loyal churchman and for many years served as Sunday school superintendent at his church.
One Sunday he gave a long and serious talk about conversion and then asked, "Are there any questions?"
One little girl popped up promptly and asked, "How much are those big dolls in the window of your store?"

[496] Good preaching is only half the battle. Good hearers are also essential. The most powerful sermon will bounce off some people like rain hitting a rock. Alfred Lord Tennyson's "Northern Farmer" said:

> I always came to his church before my Sally were dead
> And heard him a-bummin' away like a buzzard-clock over my head;

139

And I never knew what he meant, but I thought he had something to say
And I thought he said what he ought to have said, and I came away.

[497] When Henry Ward Beecher was preaching in Brooklyn, a man came up to him after a service and said, "I counted your mistakes in English today and you made exactly 20."

Beecher replied, "I bet you I made 100."

At the same service a young immigrant boy sat in a rear pew. Later that boy, grown to be Dr. Michael Pupin, noted inventor and professor at Columbia University, said of those early lonesome days, "Nothing so inspired and stimulated me as those sermons of Dr. Beecher's."

The faultfinder found 20 mistakes, but a youngster found help, hope, and inspiration.

PRIDE

[498] What's the worst of all the deadly sins? In days when life was more leisurely, monks and learned philosophers gravely debated this question. If sin ruins a person, what is its most fatal form? Many finally agreed that pride was the worst sin. John Ruskin said, "Pride is at the bottom of all great mistakes." Thomas Aquinas stated, "Pride is the most grievous of all sins, because it exceeds them all in that turning away from God that is the crowning constituent of all sin."

[499] Pride and selfishness were characteristics of Queen Elizabeth, who ruled England for half a century, and she suffered much because of them. Her favorite courtier, the Earl of Essex, took part in a plot against his political enemies and was sentenced to die. The queen was eager to pardon him, but she said, "I would save him, but only if he humbles himself and asks me to." No message came, and Essex was put to death.

From that time on, Elizabeth's heartbreak affected her health, for she could not forget Essex. One day as a lady-in-waiting to the queen lay dying, she sent for Queen Elizabeth and confessed that Essex had indeed entrusted her with a message pleading for his life and had given her his ring as proof, but that she had wanted Essex dead and had therefore never delivered the message. For Elizabeth, this knowledge was a wound from which she never recovered. She did little else for the rest of her days but mourn for Essex. Pride was her undoing.

PROGRESS

[500] Progress must be in the right direction. If I am heading for a precipice, I'd rather not get there too fast. A horse and buggy or an oxcart would suit me better than a high-powered automobile. And if I'm speeding along at 600 miles per hour, as we do on today's jetliners, I'd like some reassurance that the place I'm going to is really worth getting to that fast.

[501] Antiques gain in value as time goes by. Yesterday's junk often becomes today's collectibles, and yesterday's masterpieces are today priceless inheritances. They are worth more and mean more to us than they did to their originators. When Beethoven composed his symphonies, for example, he wrote music for instruments that were then not in existence. They had to be invented in order to produce the music, so that Beethoven can be interpreted better today than in his own time. The same is certainly true of Bach. Suppose he could have heard his works played on a magnificent modern organ or heard them performed by the Philadelphia Symphony!

[502] A sign on a building in a town on the New Jersey shore says, "We *BUY* old furniture. We *SELL* antiques."

[503] "What is progress?" Henry Thoreau demanded during a discussion with a friend.
    "Advancing from a stagecoach to a railroad train is progress," the friend responded.
    "Not necessarily," replied Thoreau. "It may just be meanness going faster."

[504] Tools have improved greatly. Galileo put together an iron pipe and two pieces of handground glass in order to see the stars more clearly, but his discoveries revolutionized astronomy. Now at

Mount Palomar in California we have a multimillion-dollar telescope with a lens 17 feet in diameter encased in a tube that's 70 feet long. But tools alone are not enough. Henry Ford said, "The machine is 10 percent in arriving at the desired results; the man is 90 percent."

[505] Roy Chapman Andrews, noted anthropologist and explorer, tells a story about the "Living Buddha" of Mongolia, the leader of millions of Buddhists. This "Living Buddha" was a man of education and of original ideas, but he had to deal routinely each day with great masses of followers and was a little bored by it all. One daily routine was the blessing of throngs of worshipers and priests who came to the temple. The "Living Buddha" decided to modernize the blessing. He installed a small electric generator and stretched a wire down the long courtyard where the faithful gathered. The pilgrims lined up to touch the wire and received a memorable blessing when the Buddha threw the switch. Andrews was invited to receive the blessing, and he could not courteously refuse. "The shock nearly knocked me over," he said.

[506] And he gave it as his opinion that whoever could make two ears of corn or two blades of grass grow on a spot of ground where only one grew before, would deserve better of mankind and do a more essential service to his country than the whole race of politicians put together.
JONATHAN SWIFT

RELIGION

[507] The important task that faces America is that of learning the direction it should go. As a guide for choosing the right path neither history nor the study of modern society shows any agency comparable with religion. Our country relies on its religious leaders to give its citizens a vision of what life should mean. Religion sees our world as working out some purpose of God, and man's place, as a child of God, in helping to carry on that purpose.
ARTHUR H. COMPTON

[508] Someone wrote of a woman that "she had just enough religion to make her miserable—too much to be happy dancing, drinking, and carrying on, and too little to be happy at a prayer meeting."

[509] When Camp Upton on Long Island was being converted into a research base to discover new uses for atomic power, representatives of the news media were invited to tour the place. Scientists guided them around, pointing out the various buildings and citing their functions. They all fitted into the atomic research program except the chapel. "We haven't found any use for the chapel," one of the scientists explained apologetically. One of the newsmen commented later, "I saw Hiroshima. Maybe they ought to use that chapel!"

[510] Too often people have the idea that religion is something to be put on to make them be good, like a straitjacket. They think it negative and confining. Yet Jesus never said "I am a wall" or "I am a fence." He spoke of himself as a door or a roadway. Of course, a door can shut you out, but it is chiefly a means of access, of coming in and going out. A roadway is intended to lead you somewhere. And religion is above all a means to make your life wider and bigger and to lead you to greater things.

[511] Many doors have four panels, two small upper panels and two larger lower panels. They form in relief a cross-shaped pattern. This style of doorway is no accident. It was fashioned intentionally by the carpenters' guilds of the Middle Ages, before the powers of the industrial age beguiled people into believing that they could make their own heaven. Those medieval carpenters took as their motto the words of Jesus, "I am the door." They deliberately wrought into every doorway the sign of the cross, marking it as the way to a fuller, larger, more abundant life.

[512] Too often we partition the world into sections. We try to separate the sacred from the secular. We carefully mark off a small area of life for religion, and some people seem to see a Keep Out! sign on that area. It's time we knew that any religion worth its salt

must permeate every area of life—church, home, factory, school, business.

[513] Sometimes I hear people ask, "Is Christianity going to survive?" Then I wonder whether such people have lost their sense of humor or their sense of history or both!
JAMES MOFFATT

[514] "Religion is not a utility but a satisfaction," said Dr. Henry Sloane Coffin. It is not a tool to prod us through this world into something presumably better, but a bringer of peace and power while we are here.

[515] Religion's worst enemy is not opposition, but indifference. Generations ago the spinning wheel stood in the middle of the living room. It was a useful and needed part of everyday life. Now a spinning wheel in the living room would at best be a conversation piece or a valued antique. Too often the reading of the Bible and the practice of religion fall into the same class—interesting ornaments from the past but of no practical value in our materialistic age.

[516] The Christian religion, properly understood, is not primarily something to be endured. It is something to be enjoyed! There is a difference, and happily so. Of course, there are demands on us. And there are obligations to be met. But over and above duty, discipline and denial is the joy that is experienced.
E. RAYMOND SHAHEEN

[517] The spirit of our age is to keep religion in its place, and that place is often a secluded corner. We hear over and over again that a person's faith is his own affair, never to be questioned. Political assemblies open with prayer and then seem to forget all about God. Schools can educate children in almost everything except morality. The place left for religion is very small and keeps shrinking. To this spirit the Bible flings down a challenge. It sets religion in the framework of world events, not as a private program for pious people but as God's plan for all humanity.

[518] Some Girl Scouts went on a hike with their leader, who was a Roman Catholic. After the hike, a religious medal that the leader wore around her neck hung out over her blouse. One of the girls said to her, "Your religion is showing." But isn't that the way it ought to be?

[519] We seem to be a very religious people. Sessions of Congress and of the state legislatures open with prayer. Most newspapers have sections on religion. Bibles are found everywhere, in homes and hotel rooms. Thousands of religious books are published every year, and more than a thousand religious periodicals flourish. The religious beliefs of political candidates are big news. If Paul came here as he did to Athens, he would say again, "I perceive you Americans are very religious." But here as in Athens, Paul might look more deeply with his keen insight at our way of life. He would find that behind the facade of religion are pornographic books, magazines, and movies; corruption and immorality in politics; a million divorces in a single year. He would wonder how we can have so much religion and so little of its power in our lives.

[520] The essence of religion is love born out of faith. Ethics and philosophy are important adjuncts to religion, but never enough in themselves. On the ship of life, philosophy is the paint job. It dresses it up and makes it look nice. Ethics can be the rudder of the ship, but a rudder is useless unless the hull is sound and the engine operates. Religion offers the strength of a sound hull and the motive power to operate the ship. That power comes from love.

REMEMBRANCE

[521] Good things have to be engraved on our memories; the bad ones often stick there by themselves.

[522] Blessings we enjoy daily; and for most of them, because they are so common, most men forget to pay their praise. But let us not forget, for it is a sacrifice so pleasing to him that made the sun and us and gives us flowers and showers and meat and content.
Izaak Walton

[523] Memory is a wonderful faculty of the mind. However, suppose you remembered every detail of life—every old telephone number, address, baseball score, every miscellaneous fact that came to you? Fortunately, our minds store these things away in some deep cellar of the brain where they don't constantly intrude on our consciousness. Dr. William Ludwig, psychology professor at Wagner College, used to say, "The greatest ability of the mind is remembering; but the second greatest is forgetting."

[524] The Campbell clan massacred the MacDonald clan in a battle at Glencoe in western Scotland in 1692, and the feud has simmered ever since. Recently a man named MacDonald came to Scotland on a holiday from the United States, and a party was given in his honor. At the party he was introduced to a man named Campbell, but he refused to shake hands because of what the Campbells had done to the MacDonalds at Glencoe.

"But that's an old story, something that happened almost 300 years ago and should be forgotten," protested the Campbell.

"That may be so," answered MacDonald, "but I only heard about it yesterday." So old hatreds and prejudice live on!

[525] In 1906 earthquake and fire destroyed the library of the Institute for Arts and Sciences in San Francisco. In far-off Leipzig, Germany, a young scientist knew that books would be needed, so he packed two cartons of precious scientific books and sent them to San Francisco to replace those that had been destroyed. Forty years later he was an old man, bombed out and left destitute. Timidly he wrote to the Institute in San Francisco. Did anyone remember him? Could anyone send help? The librarian at the Institute was a lady 86 years of age. She remembered well the books that came in 1906 and how valuable they were. So four cases of food and clothing were quickly gathered and sent overseas to the aged scientist who had become a victim of war's depradations. Kindness and love know no boundaries of time and space.

RESOURCES, INNER STRENGTH

[526] Often the invisible, inward resources are what really count. You might have two clocks, one a child's toy and the other the

product of fine craftsmanship. Set the hands of both clocks at the same hour, and outwardly both would seem alike. Yet one would have no inner resources. It would tell the right time for one minute, but at every other minute of the day it would be wrong.

[527] When John Wesley returned to England after failing in his missionary efforts in Georgia—or so he thought—he felt depressed and believed that God's power was no longer in his life. Troubled, he wandered one night into a mission meeting in Aldersgate where he heard a Moravian minister read Luther's powerful introduction to the epistle to the Romans, which expressed Luther's belief about justification by faith and the change which God works in human lives through such faith. Said Wesley, "I felt I did trust in Christ and an assurance was given me that he has taken away my sins, even mine, and saved me from the law of sin and death." By this thought, Wesley added, "My heart was strangely warmed."

[528] Even in these days of nuclear energy, hydroelectric power remains the most reliable source. Niagara Falls, for example, helps provide light and power for much of Ontario and for sections of New York State. What makes this possible is the accident of nature that placed Lake Erie 169 feet higher than Lake Ontario. If both lakes were on the same level, there'd be no source of power. It's somewhat the same in our lives. If everything is on our own level, we can do much less than when we can draw down power from above.

[529] Martin Luther and his associate Philip Melanchthon were caught in a severe storm while on a journey that was to take them across the Elbe River in northern Germany. They found the river turbulent and swollen, and the little ferry boat looked unsafe. "We had better not cross now, for the stars are against us," Melanchthon said. But Luther answered, "We are the Lord's—so we are lords over the stars also."

REWARDS

[530] Whether or not we get the credit for some achievement, we have a duty to do our best. There was disagreement about who

deserved credit for the Allied victory at the Marne in World War I, and some reporters asked Field Marshal Joffre of France about it. "I don't know who deserves credit for the victory," he said. "But I know that if it had been a defeat, they would have blamed it on me."

[531] A retired minister was invited to conduct the services at a village church. He took his little grandson with him, and as they entered the church, the minister took a bill from his wallet and placed it in the offering plate. After the service one of the ushers came to him and said, "It's our custom to offer the visiting preacher whatever is placed on the offering plate. We found this bill on the plate and we want you to have it."

Solemnly the minister took back his own bill and put it into his pocket, while the little boy watched in astonishment. As they were walking homeward, the lad said, "Gee, Grandpa, if you'd put more into that you would have gotten more out of it!"

SCIENCE

[532] *Original version:*

Twinkle, twinkle, little star,
How I wonder what you are,
Up above the world so high,
Like a diamond in the sky!

Revised version:

Twinkle, twinkle, giant star,
I know exactly what you are:
An incandescent ball of gas
Condensing to a solid mass.
Twinkle, twinkle, giant star,
I need not wonder what you are;
For, seen by spectroscopic ken
You're helium and hydrogen.

SOURCE UNKNOWN

[533] Some time ago a Chicago family made a startling discovery. They had lived for four years on the second floor of a two-family dwelling. There was a trapdoor on the floor of the living room with

148

a rug covering it. One day during housecleaning the rug was removed, and the father of the family yielded to curiosity and pried open the door, hoping to find some hidden treasure, or jewelry, or hundred-dollar bills. Instead, he found four sticks of dynamite, enough to blow the building to pieces! For four years that family had played, slept, worked, and watched television only a few feet away from a destructive force that could have blown them to kingdom come. But isn't that an apt parable for our world today? We go on with our everyday chores, while our whole world is close to great forces that could destroy everything.

[534] An incident at an airline counter in Philadelphia shows how our age takes miracles for granted. The clerk picked up the telephone and heard the caller ask, "How long does it take to go from Philadelphia to Phoenix?"

Because the clerk was busy with a customer and would have to look up the answer, she said, "Just a minute."

As she was about to put down the phone, the clerk heard the caller say "Thank you" and hang up.

[535] Our new knowledge of space is not an ego builder. Suppose there are dozens of other worlds and other universes: how unimportant we become. But long before space exploration began, Tennyson wrote of the immensity of heaven and the puny insignificance of mankind. "What is it all but the murmur of gnats in the gleam of a million million suns?" he asked. And long before Tennyson, the psalmist wrote, "When I look at thy heavens, the work of thy fingers . . . what is man that thou art mindful of him?" (Ps. 8:3-4). But the psalmist knew that God was mindful, and that made all the difference!

[536] The power at our disposal today baffles the imagination. Once a single horse was enough to take churchgoers to church. Now we come in machines that have under their hoods the power of hundreds of horses. The first automobile I owned had three lights—two in front and a red one at the rear. Now a modern car has 33 lights! And my grandmother was a better cook than most cooks today, using a stove that had one small wood fire in it. How puzzled she would

be by a modern electric kitchen with all its gadgets. Yet today we are at the mercy of machines and power sources. If a single wire falls due to a storm, we can't see, heat the house, preserve our food, tell time, and perhaps can't even open a door!

[537] It is not without significance that capable scientists of today tend to be devoutly religious, whereas many of those who claimed to be scientists only a generation ago took pride in proclaiming themselves to be either agnostics or atheists, for they could not correlate religion and science. We of today are so much better informed than our fellows of generations ago that we have enough perspective to recognize our insignificance in the divine order.
WILLARD H. DOW

[538] We live now in a grisly morning-after. Science has improved our means of achieving deterioration.
ALDOUS HUXLEY

[539] In his book *Worlds in Collision,* Immanuel Velikovsky studies from a scientific standpoint two biblical stories—the great flood and the incident of Joshua commanding the sun to stand still. He finds very similar stories in the traditions of China, India, Egypt, and the Aztec civilization of America. Since there is no known connection between these traditions, the stories are likely to have their origin in fact, Velikovsky concludes.

SERVICE

[540] A young man complained to a minister about the injustice and evil in the world. He blamed God for the whole mess and said, "I could make a better world than this myself."

Quietly the minister responded, "Good! Go to it! That's exactly what God put you into the world to do."

[541] I don't know what your destiny will be, but one thing I know: the only ones among you who will be really happy are those who have sought and found a way to serve.
ALBERT SCHWEITZER

[542] During a Civil War battle a young officer became detached from his regiment and could not find his way back to it. As he searched for his comrades, he met General Philip Sheridan and asked, "Where shall I step in? I've become detached from my regiment."

Sheridan roared in reply, "Step in? Step in anywhere! There's fighting all along the line." So in service to humanity there are opportunities everywhere—at home, at work, in the neighborhood. Step in anywhere!

[543] God does not say, "Work hard and earn your way to heaven." God gives us heaven as a free gift of grace and then expects us to live up to our responsibilities.

[544] To any sensitive conscience, unemployment or enforced idleness can be troubling. Too much needs to be done if this world is to be made a better place. Idleness deserves the sharp rebuke given in the opening scene of Shakespeare's *Julius Caesar,* when the Roman tribune chides the loafers in the marketplace:

Is this a holiday? What, know you not,
Being mechanical, you ought not walk
Upon a laboring day without the sign
Of your profession? . . . Be gone!
Run to your houses, fall upon you knees,
Pray to the gods to intermit the plague
That needs must light on this ingratitude!

Christians also sometimes wander around without the "sign of their profession." When we pray that God's will be done, we need to add that God's will be done by us also. We can never say, "Let George do it," or "Let the minister do it." We are God's workers in the world.

[545] If you were working by candlelight and the candle was burning down, you'd hurry to finish your job. But the candle of life grows shorter daily for each of us. The epitaph on Cecil Rhodes'

tomb in South Africa carries a message that applies to our lives: "So much to do; so little done."

[546] A person who comes to church once a year is likely to find the service strange and will probably say that church does nothing for him. On the other hand, a faithful worshiper who comes every week, sings in the choir, helps teach, and takes a turn visiting the sick and shut-ins is likely to say that the church is the sustaining force in his life. Only when people trust enough and dare enough to plunge deeply into something do they get their fullest reward.

[547] Through this toilsome world, alas!
Once and only once I'll pass.
If a kindness I may show,
If a good deed I may do,
Let me do it while I can.
No delay! For it is plain
I shall not pass this way again.
An Old Epitaph

[548] People can always find excuses. The priest and Levite who passed by the wounded stranger on the Jericho Road may have thought up many good reasons for not helping: *This man is a stranger . . . This is dangerous country . . . We have more important things to do . . . We need our money for other things . . . We're too weak and tired to help now . . . We're not responsible for this man . . . He probably would not thank us even if we helped him . . . Maybe he's in a conspiracy with the robbers and they'll attack us . . . Probably he was reckless and deserved the trouble he got into . . . Somebody better able to help will come along soon . . . He looks too far gone and he might die and I'll get blamed.*

Those are only a few of the excuses that people can think up for not helping others. Fortunately for the wounded stranger, along came a good Samaritan whose only thought was, "What would I want done for me under the same circumstances?"

SHEEP AND SHEPHERDS

[549] The Bible often depicts the masses as sheep and their leaders as shepherds. This comparison had meaning in an agrarian society, but unfortunately sheep are rather dumb. They never learn tricks; their shaggy coats get caught in briars; they wander off and can't find their way back; they are defenseless against their enemies. They have two virtues, however: they faithfully follow a leader, and they rarely show bad temper. No wonder humanity is compared to sheep!

[550] Once I watched a flock of sheep being driven down a country road. At the side of the road was an old farmhouse with an open porch. One sheep, who seemed to be in front of the flock, suddenly left the road and ran up over the porch and down the other side. All the other sheep then took the same detour.

[551] Shepherds are a mystery to modern urbanites. If a person is a policeman, storekeeper, or clerk, we can form a definite picture of what he does, but for most of us information about shepherds comes secondhand. Yet in old Palestine, a shepherd was part of the community and often an important and honored person. Moses, David, Amos, and other national heroes were shepherds. Living much of the time away from other people, out in the fields, they had special rights and privileges. Their sheep and cattle represented wealth. To be a shepherd was to rank highly in Palestinian society.

[552] In biblical times shepherds had to be courageous. To neglect or abandon a flock was unthinkable. Facing danger from wild animals, storms, or foul weather was among a shepherd's normal duties, which also included climbing steep hillsides and carrying injured sheep safely back to the fold. This kind of courage is evidently expected in the Christian ministry, for the word *pastor* means shepherd.

[553] Sheep are loyal to the shepherd who leads them, and they like to stay close together in a flock, but they are thoughtless. If the grass is sweet, a sheep will nibble away and wander off. Many human beings are like that. They are basically loyal and do not

intend to go astray, but they follow their appetites and inclinations without foresight or planning, wandering from one tuft of grass to another until they are hopelessly lost.

SIN

[554] Some people make the mistake of wishing that life could be wrapped in plastic—pure, protected, uncontaminated. Wouldn't this be wonderful? The answer is, no. Overprotected children or hothouse plants suffer when exposed to normal conditions. "A world where we could not sin would be hell; a world where we would not sin would be heaven."

[555] A college student discovered that he needed a Bible for a course in religion and wrote home asking that his Bible be sent to him. His father wrapped it carefully and took it to the post office to mail to the student.

The clerk took the package and shook it. "Anything in here that can be broken?" he asked.

"Only the Ten Commandments," the father replied.

[556] An artist wanted to paint a picture of the prodigal son but had trouble finding a model who looked dissolute enough. Finally he went down to skid row and saw a dirty, unkempt man in ragged clothes. "I will pay you well if you will come to my studio tomorrow and let me paint you," he told the drifter. The next day the man arrived, cleanly shaven and neatly dressed. The artist sadly turned away. "I can't use you now," he said. "I wanted you to come just as you were." When God calls us, he wants us just as we are. If people are saintly and perfect, they have no need for a Savior. Jesus said, "I have not come to call the righteous, but sinners to repentance" (Luke 5:32).

[557] Falling into sin doesn't condemn anybody, but staying in it does. A visitor at a fishing dock asked an old fisherman who was sitting there, "If I were to fall into this water, would I drown?"

It was a queer way of asking how deep the water was, but the fisherman had a good answer. "Naw," he said. "Fallin' into the water doesn't drown anybody. It's staying under it that does."

[558] Sins do not become virtues by being widely practiced. Right is still right if nobody is right. Wrong is still wrong if everybody is wrong. Some have contended that sex aberrations are as common as the common cold, but nobody so far has asked us to consider that the cold is normal and desirable.
FULTON J. SHEEN

[559] Sin is an obvious fact today. The world is full of it. Every newspaper, magazine, radio, or television newscast, all literature from ancient times to Shakespeare to the latest modern novel, tells of sins ranging from angry thoughts to pride, deceit, greed, selfishness, envy, stealing, and murder. Like Hamlet, we can all say, "I am myself indifferent honest, but yet I could accuse me of such crimes that it were better my mother had not borne me."

[560] Many have puzzled themselves about the origin of evil. I observe that there is evil, and that there is a way to escape it, and with this I begin and end.
JOHN NEWTON

[561] In the town of Pelham, New York, is Split Rock Road, which takes its name from a natural wonder. A tiny seed took root in a crevice in a huge boulder. Quietly and unnoticed it grew and gained strength. Finally the product of the seed was stronger than the boulder, and the rock was split in two, with the tree still growing between the sections. It's an example of how the weak things of the world can overcome the strong—at least sometimes— and how the power of good can overcome evil.

STEWARDSHIP

[562] "Like a mighty army moves the Church of God," we sing in the hymn "Onward, Christian Soldiers." Anyone who's lived through a major war may think that line rather funny. When a great army moves, it levies billions of dollars in taxes and gets them. It

builds ships by the hundreds, assigns young men and women to jobs they never expected, requisitions factories, shifts millions of people from one place to another, builds cities almost overnight, and takes over transportation systems. We may sing it loud and long, but we would need an undreamed-of standard of loyalty to God to make that line believable.

[563] "Everything belongs to God and we are only his stewards and caretakers," a minister said in a sermon one Sunday.

The next day a well-to-do member of the congregation drove the pastor around his 100-acre estate. "Come on now, pastor," he teased. "Does this place belong to me or doesn't it?"

The minister responded, "If you'll ask me that question 100 years from now, I'll give you a definite answer."

[564] Some principles of stewardship:

1. God is a creator and therefore owner of all things.

2. We are stewards and caretakers and must give account for what is entrusted to us.

3. God's ownership and human stewardship must be acknowledged.

4. Such acknowledgement requires as a material expression setting aside a fair portion of income as an act of worship.

5. This portion ought to be administered systematically for the advancement of God's kingdom and work.

[565] What I had, I lost.
What I saved, I spent.
What I gave, I have.

[566] Sometimes we delude ourselves about true values. An Arab lost his way in the desert, and for two days and nights he had no food or water. Intense heat during the day and cold nights left him weakened and fearing death. Finally he stumbled across a caravan route and followed it to a campground where some travelers had recently stayed. He searched and searched for a morsel of food and was momentarily exhilarated when he found a bag with something round and hard in it. Could it be nuts or dried fruit? He tore the

bag open, then threw it down in disgust. "It is only pearls," he cried, sinking down onto the sand to perish.

[567] "The church is always asking for money," some people complain. The reason is that it never has enough. There's too much work to be done, and our resources are too small. We need not be apologetic in any way about calling on people to exercise good stewardship in providing for the work of the church. Giving is an essential part of the Christian life. List the biblical references to giving and stewardship, and you'll fill many pages. *Giving* is mentioned at least 700 times in the Bible, *sacrifice* 300 times, *money* more than 100 times.

[568] "Investigate before you invest" is good advice even in charitable giving. On a busy street corner in a midwestern city some college students set up a booth with a sign reading, "Give generously! Help the widow of the Unknown Soldier." Passersby contributed quite a bit of money before someone caught on to the hoax.

[569] Be careful when you talk about a "widow's mite," as if that were a paltry gift. One man learned this the hard way. A visitor came to him from his church during an annual financial appeal, and the man, who was quite wealthy, jovially agreed to contribute. "I'll add my widow's mite," he said.

"Do you really mean that?" asked the visitor. "Like the widow in the Bible?"

"Of course I mean it," the man responded.

"We couldn't take that much," said the visitor, "So I'll just put you down for $100,000."

Indignantly the man sputtered, "Is this your idea of a joke? What do you mean?"

"If you'll look it up in your Bible," said the visitor, "You'll find that the widow gave all that she had."

[570] Money can buy delicious food but not appetite. Money can pay for doctors but cannot buy health. Money can attract flatterers and hire servants but not friends. Money can buy a big funeral, but not mourners. Things like peace and happiness and satisfaction

cannot be bought. The deepest needs of the soul are not touched by money or goods or things or possessions.

[571] If God is important in our lives, we cannot give him half-hearted leftovers of our time, talents, and money. Suppose you invited a guest for dinner—some prominent person—and then when all were seated at the table you said to him, "You must wait. When we've finished, we'll scrape the plates and you can have what's left." Your guest would be indignant and insulted. The proper procedure is to offer the guest the first and best portion.

Some people are very polite at dinner. They even start the meal by inviting God, perhaps in the old prayer, "Come, Lord Jesus, be our guest." But when it actually comes down to the nitty-gritty, they give God what's left over—scraps of time, minutes they don't know what else to do with; scraps of their mind, for they know a mass of secular statistics but little of the Bible; scraps of their money, small change they can easily spare.

[572] A visitor who was being shown around New York commented on the crowds and noise in the subway. His host said, "At the next station we will change to an express train. That will save us two minutes."

Said the bewildered visitor, "And what shall we do with those two minutes?"

[573] To pledge or not to pledge; that is the question.
Whether 'tis nobler in a man
To take the gospel free and let another foot the bill,
Or sign a pledge and pay toward church expenses.
To give, to pay—aye, there's the rub! To pay,
When on a free-pew plan a man may have
A sitting free and take the gospel, too,
As though he paid, and none be aught the wiser,
Save the finance committee, who—
Most honorable of men—can keep a secret.
To err is human, and human too, to buy
At cheapest rate. I'll take the gospel so!
For others do the same—a common rule.

I'm wise, I'll wait, not work. I'll pray, not pay,
And let the other fellow foot the bills
And so I'll get the gospel free, you see!
With apologies to Shakespeare

[574] A lot of our giving is like Farmer Applegate's cow. Asked how much milk the cow gave, the farmer answered, "If you mean willingly, not a drop. But if you corner her in her stall, you can take about 10 quarts from her."

[575] Someone asked, "What does 'Amen' mean?"
   He was told, "It means, 'Yes, Lord, I'm for it, and I'll stand my share of the expenses.' "

[576] It's not what you'd do with a million,
If a million should e'er be your lot,
But what are you doing at present
With the buck and a half that you've got.

[577] Some delightful toys were created by the Victorians a century ago. One metal toy included an old woman at a washtub, a windmill, a mason with a trowel, and a big rooster with movable wings perched atop a fence. It was an elaborate contrivance, but what made it work? The trick was to put a coin into a slot in the toy. Then the woman would scrub, the mason wield his trowel, the windmill turn, and the rooster flap his wings. Amusing as it may seem, the same principle works in church. God forbid that we should give just to see the wheels go around, but without giving nothing can happen.

[578] Nobody is completely self-made and self-sufficient. Some may boast that they don't owe anything to anybody, but they are deceiving themselves. We all owe so much that it's embarrassing. We're in debt to our parents for life itself. We're in debt to society for electricity, indoor plumbing, telephones, televisions, and every other thing that was created by someone else's brains and inventive genius. We're in debt to our government, whether we like it or not, and sometimes young people are forced to pay this debt with years

given to military service. And we're in debt to God, for we are only stewards or caretakers of the earth, and one day our accounts will be audited.

SUCCESS

[579] The best formula for getting a product across successfully may lie in these few lines from a sales letter:

Early to bed, early to rise,
Work like hell and advertise.

[580] John Wesley's motto for success: "At it; all at it; always at it."

[581] Someone asked Henry Ward Beecher for the secret of the success of his pastorate in a Brooklyn church. He replied, "I have 500 hearers who repeat on Monday what I said on Sunday." That's the kind of support that makes a ministry successful.

[582] I know of one who became a person of large doings because on a certain day he wore, by accident, the wrong pair of trousers. Consequently, on that day, instead of trotting all about the office as usual, he remained assiduously at his desk with the incongruent pantaloons well hidden. He summoned to him all those from whom he required information, even asking the head of the firm, by telephone, to stop in when he went by. He discovered at the end of the day that he had dispatched more business than he usually did in a week; he wasted no time in genial to-and-fro; he strongly impressed valuable customers by not rising from his chair. He remained bashfully at his desk until all his colleagues had gone home, and so happened to catch an important long-distance call. He specialized at staying at his desk thereafter. By sitting still, he rose to the top of the tree. It was the sheer hazard of the wrong pair of trousers.
CHRISTOPHER MORLEY

[583] I hate to be a kicker; I always long for peace,
But the wheel that does the squeaking is the wheel that gets the grease.

It's nice to be a peaceful soul and not too hard to please,
But the dog that keeps on scratching is the dog that gets the fleas.
Now don't get any notions that are harmful in your head,
But the baby that keeps yelling is the baby that gets fed.

TEACHERS

[584] An epitaph on a teacher's tomb near Oxford University reads, "He loved great things and thought little of himself, desiring neither fame nor influence. He won the devotion of many and was a power in their lives. Seeking no disciples, he taught to many the greatness of the world and of man's mind." The same words could apply to a multitude of faithful teachers.

[585] A good teacher is a guide and a light bringer. In my early days at school, promotion from one grade to another was based on skill in reading, so I moved ahead rapidly. However, my knowledge of arithmetic did not keep up, and I was completely baffled when confronted with algebra. Then one day a kindly teacher called me aside and explained carefully from the very beginning how it worked. It was like the sun bursting from behind a cloud! Once I understood the basics, the whole thing became clear.

[586] Gems of storytelling called parables were often used by Jesus to emphasize or explain his teachings. It's still the method of a good teacher. Every preacher or public speaker knows the value of a pertinent story or illustration. Among the 38 parables or stories in the New Testament, many are so famous they seem to be part of history.

[587] Good teachers are more concerned about the future development of their charges than about immediate results. Teachers don't hand their pupils an already-lighted candle, which could soon burn out, but they prefer to show them how to light a thousand candles. Suppose you visited a friend's home and found there was no light. You could strike a match or light a candle, but either would soon burn out. Or you could stretch an electric cable over the hills, wire the house, and install electric lights. Then even when you were far

away your friend could flick a switch and flood his house with light. So it is with teaching. Teachers are not satisfied to hand their pupils a lighted match, which may help for a moment, but rather wire their house of learning for electricity so they can achieve lifelong benefits.

TEMPTATION

[588] A temptation to do something harmful or wrong is never really overcome until you have the strength to face it without giving in. To try to withdraw into a shell or to retreat from the world is not victory, but defeat. An alcoholic, for instance, can sometimes be rescued by an agency like Alcoholics Anonymous and returned to normal life. But the rescue effort is not complete until that person is able to be in the company of drinkers, perhaps with a bottle or glass in front of him, and still have the willpower to resist the temptation. Then the cure is successful and that person can be trusted to resist, because he has protection wherever he goes.

[589] If a child is playing with a toy you don't want him to have, how can you get it away from him? Take it by force, and he'll bawl for hours. The better way is to distract his attention by interesting him in something else. Then while his attention is diverted, you can take away the toy. Oddly enough, that's exactly how the devil tempts us. The lure of wealth or fame or pleasure distracts us and lets him take from our hearts our trust in God.

[590] You cannot prevent the birds from flying overhead, but you can stop them from nesting in your hair.
MARTIN LUTHER

[591] Three men responded to an advertisement placed for a bus driver. The interviewer asked each the same question: "How close could you drive to the edge of a precipice?"

The first applicant said, "I keep tight control of the wheel. I could get within six inches."

Trying to outdo him, the second applicant said, "I could probably get within two or three inches."

The third one said, "I don't know, because I'd keep as far on the other side of the road as possible."

[592] When something terrible happens—the kind of thing we call a holocaust, catastrophe, or disaster—we are driven to our knees and often say, "It's in the hand of God." Insurance policies usually describe such awful things as "acts of God." Such things we turn over to God, but the little things we think we can handle ourselves. Yet a cruel form of torture involves little drops of water constantly dripping on a chained victim. Little things can drive us to distraction and cause great trouble. You would not be likely to run into a stone wall, but you can easily stub your toe or trip over a brick lying in your path.

THANKSGIVING

[593] As the American moves farther and farther away from the soil, the reality of Thanksgiving fades into a pale symbol buried beneath an elaborate ceremonial of gastronomics.
Fannie Hurst

[594] During World War II, Fairfax Downey penned some lines that remind us of our need for constant thanksgiving:

Thank Thee, Lord, for this my bed,
For roof unbombed above my head
And for Thy gift, my daily bread.
Why is it we must come to know
Belatedly, from other's woe,
The gratitude we always owe?

[595] If anyone should give me a dish of sand and tell me there were particles of iron in it, I might look for them with my eyes and search for them with my clumsy fingers, and be unable to find them. But let me take a magnet and sweep through it, and how it would draw to itself the most invisible particles by the sheer power of attraction. The unthankful heart, like my fingers in the sand, discovers no blessings; but let the thankful heart sweep through the day, and as the magnet finds the iron, so it will find in every

163

hour some blessings; only the iron in God's hand is gold.
OLIVER WENDELL HOLMES

[596] There was a time when faith began to slip,
When I had lost all that I had to lose—
Or so it seemed to me. I lost home,
My job—I had no house, no food, no shoes.
Then suddenly I felt ashamed,
For I, who talked of shoes
Then chanced to meet
Upon the busy highway of my life
A man who had no feet.

[597] For all things beautiful, and good, and true;
For things that seemed not good yet turned to good;
For all the sweet compulsions of Thy will
That chased, and tried, and wrought us to Thy shape;
For things unnumbered that we take of right,
And value first when first they are withheld;
For light and air; sweet sense of sound and smell;
For ears to hear the heavenly harmonies;
For eyes to see the unseen in the seen;
For vision of The Worker in the work;
For hearts that apprehend Thee everywhere;
   We thank Thee, Lord!
JOHN OXENHAM

[598] Before the days of the welfare state, a wealthy man gave a
poor family the money they needed for an operation to save the
life of one of their children. The recipients were very grateful and
told the man, "We'll tell him about his benefactor, and he'll thank
you all the days of his life."

But the man replied, "Nonsense! You don't thank the clouds for
the rain. Teach him to thank God."

[599] Once I found a nickel in the sand at the beach and thought
myself lucky. I searched through the sand, hoping to find more
treasure, but was not successful. Then I saw a man with a magnetic

device on the end of a stick, which he used to draw metal objects out of the sand. He told me he often found coins and sometimes even jewelry. What it taught me is that we can search through life without getting much from it, but a thankful heart can be like that magnetic device. It draws the best things out of life.

TIME

[600] It's disappointing to find that January 1 is often just about like December 31. Life doesn't follow a calendar. For convenience, business firms close their books at the end of the year and start a new ledger in January, but for most of us there are likely to be bigger changes and newer beginnings in April or September. As a boy, I used to wonder about the next day, especially on New Year's Eve. Would the world change suddenly at midnight? It was always a surprise to find that 12:01 A.M. was exactly like 11:59 P.M. If I hadn't watched the clock I would not have known that it was a new year.

[601] Fifty years is a short time in history, but a long time in a person's life. Measure back 50 years in society or in economics or in science, and the amount of change is startling. There was no television, no atomic bomb, no computer, very little commercial aviation, and John D. Rockefeller handed out dimes as great favors. Fifty years ago you could buy a fairly good house for $4990. The trouble is that thinking about things past doesn't help us today. We need to know what's happening now.

[602] Life is a book in chapters three:
The past, the present, and "yet-to-be."
The first is written and laid away,
The second we're writing day by day.
The last but not least of these chapters three
Is locked from our sight. Only God holds the key.

[603] After the death of an elderly aunt, we had to prepare her house for sale by cleaning out things that had accumulated over the years. One chest of drawers was full of doilies, napkins, and

tablecloths, most of them with lace borders carefully and beautifully crocheted. We thought of the countless hours of effort that our aunt and her two sisters must have spent in the creation of these things. But what else did a young girl do 70 years ago? There was no radio or television, and motion pictures and phonographs were in their infancy. If a girl were really wild, she played hearts or pinochle in the evening, but if she was well-behaved, she read or crocheted.

[604] An American test pilot was trying out a new high-speed airplane and took off across the Atlantic. It seemed only minutes before he was over Europe, and he began to wonder about his speed. He radioed a ground station, asking "How fast am I going?"

The reply came in German: "You're going 6000 miles per hour."

"That can't be right," the pilot said. "Check it out again."

This time the reply came in Russian: "We've checked it out, and that's right."

"Good Lord!" said the pilot.

This time the reply came, "Yes, son?"

[605] Life is transient, but spiritual things endure. The water that today flows past New York City in the Hudson River was yesterday at Poughkeepsie and the day before that was at Albany. Tomorrow the water will have flowed into the ocean, but the river will still be there. So time, "like an ever flowing stream, bears all its sons away." We live out our little day, but spiritual things endure.

[606] On the back of an old grandfather clock these words were written:

When as a child I laughed and wept, time crept.
When as a youth I dreamed and talked, time walked.
When I became a full-grown man, time ran.
And later, as I older grew, time flew.
Soon I shall find, while traveling on, time gone.

[607] My birthday! What a different sound
That word had in my youthful ears;
And how each time the day comes 'round
Less and less bright its mark appears.

166

[608] "What time is it?" The person who is asked that question normally glances at a watch or clock and responds. But if that person is on the East Coast of the United States, his answer is wrong for most of the country. In Chicago it is one hour earlier; in Hawaii seven hours earlier. Time is a man-made invention and not nearly so important as it seems. Probably the only absolute about time is the adage on an old sundial: "Traveler, it is later than you think."

UNITY

[609] Unity and common purpose are hard to find anywhere in the world. Despite its name, the United Nations is far from united; rarely has there been a unanimous decision on any major item. Statesmen build walls and erect barriers around their countries, and the world is divided by curtains of iron or bamboo. Even in a Christian congregation people of diverse ideas, backgrounds, and beliefs come together, and one wonders what common purpose they possess. What draws a congregation together? There's just one common interest: the unifying force is their faith. It provides a core of purpose for their varied lives and enables them to work together in harmony.

[610] The preacher in a small country congregation was vehement on the subject of Christian unity. "When I say Christian, I mean Baptist; and when I say Baptist, I mean Bible-believing Baptist; and by Bible-believing, I mean born again in the Spirit; and by that I mean to have the Spirit indwelling. And the only place we got that is right here in this church!"

[611] During his brief term Pope John XXIII had an audience with a group of Jewish leaders. The visitors may indeed have felt ill at ease coming into the private rooms of the Vatican, but the pope set their fears to rest promptly. With extended arms, he welcomed them saying, "I am Joseph, your brother."

[612] The Arabian Nights fable of Sinbad the sailor describes a magnetic rock in the Indian Ocean that draws all the nails and bolts out of passing ships until the ships collapse and sink. In a

sense the passing of time and the distracting influences of the world loosen the nails and bolts that hold us together in families and communities. We need constant renewal to tighten up the unity of fellowship and the ties of faith.

[613] Watching a symphony orchestra perform can help us understand the need for accepting our place in life and doing our best with it. The violinists may fiddle furiously throughout an entire selection, the cymbals crash only once or twice, the soft woodwinds are barely heard, while the brasses blare out from time to time, yet all form part of a beautiful whole. If the cymbals dominated the entire piece, it would be horrible noise. If it were all violins, it would be unbalanced. All must fit in together, playing their parts. For the skinny little piccolo to envy the big fat tuba or for the bass viol to covet the violin's part would not be useful. Harmony comes only with the blending of a variety of gifts—if all are playing in the same key and playing the same piece.

VISION

[614] Part of the gloom in life comes because people don't have the faith and hope to look on the brighter side. They claim that God is unjust, life is unfair, and that their troubles are greater than anyone else's, when actually they have little to complain about. Joseph Turner, the English landscape painter, was noted for his gorgeous sunsets—all blue and purple and red and orange.

One day a woman criticized his painting, saying, "I've never seen a sunset like that."

Turner answered, "Ah, madam, but don't you wish you could?"

[615] A woman writer had trouble with her eyes and went to seek medical help. The doctor examined her carefully and then said, "When you are reading or writing, leave your desk every hour or so and go to the window and look out across the fields or at a distant tree for a few minutes. Then you'll find you can return to your desk and carry on your work." That kind of far-distant view is what we all need, a chance to turn from our narrow range of vision and look to God.

[616] Even if you have 20/20 vision, you can see only a fraction of the splendor that's around you. There are ranges of color that our physical eyes cannot perceive. For instance, we see a spectrum from red to violet, yet beyond red is infrared, beyond violet is ultraviolet, and so on in great unimaginable reaches that we never perceive because of our physical limitations. The same is true of the inner eye of the soul. We see a little of God's glory, but at best it's a tiny fraction of God's whole kingdom.

[617] Years ago American farmers faced a great problem with wheat rust, which ruined crops and led to abandoned farms and food scarcity. But Mark Carleton in Kansas and Angus McKay in Canada worked with agricultural experimenters in Russia and other parts of the world, patiently developing a strain of wheat that would resist the deadly rust. By crossbreeding various types, they finally solved the problem, and today our wheat belt can feed the world. We take this sort of thing for granted, but what happens to this resourcefulness when we deal with spiritual things? We need to apply intelligent faith and imagination diligently in our efforts to solve the world's problems.

[618] As I've watched construction work, I've been impressed by steelworkers who can calmly walk along girders only a few inches wide and many stories above the street. These daring workers don't even have a net underneath them, as tightrope walkers at a circus often do. Once I asked one of them what made it possible for him and his co-workers to be so nonchalant while doing dangerous work. "You get used to it," he said. "At first the rule is don't ever look down or around. Keep your eye on the place you are walking toward. Then you don't get frightened." It sounds like a good idea for us all, because we tend to get panicky in this uncertain world. Keep your eye on your goal, looking beyond the depths and troubles of this life.

[619] As I looked out through the window of my hotel room, the small town appeared to be a drab and ugly place. Even the sunshine seemed faint. Later when I walked out of the hotel, I found that it was really a bright and cheerful day. The fault was not with

the town or the atmosphere, but with the window, which made everything look gloomy. But doesn't that happen often in our outlook on life? The fault lies in our vision.

[620] A couple decided to sell their house and called in a realtor who carefully inspected the place. "I'll put an advertisement in the paper tomorrow and you'll get prompt action," he promised.

The next day the homeowners were out early to buy the newspaper and see the ad. It was a well-stated description of the advantages and good points of their house. The couple read it over and talked it over and then made a rush for the telephone. "We've changed our minds," they told the realtor. "We don't want to sell this place, for we'll never find another like it. We just didn't realize how many good points it had until we read your ad."

Count your blessings! You may cry out like the psalmist, "What shall I render to the Lord for all his bounty to me?" (Ps. 116:12)

[621] At a seminar for corporate executives, the instructor placed a large sheet of white paper on the wall and then marked a small black spot on it. "Now I want you to describe to me exactly what you see," he told the students.

There was an uneasy silence until one after another of the group raised a hand. They all had the same answer: "I see a small black spot."

"That's your trouble," the instructor said. "You all say you see a small black spot, and none of you mentions the large white paper."

[622] A teacher often remarked in his lectures, "When I was walking in my garden, this thought came to me. . . ." His students formed the impression that their teacher had a large and beautiful garden. But one day a few of them were invited to visit the teacher's home and were surprised to discover that the garden was really a small, narrow, fenced-in backyard. "Is this the wonderful garden you're always talking about?" they asked. "It seems so small and narrow."

"But look up and see how high it is," the teacher responded. "It reaches up to the sky."

[623] An old Hindu asked his son to bring him an apple. He cut the apple, took out a seed, split it in half, and asked his son, "What do you see?" The boy saw only an apple seed and answered, "Nothing. I see nothing." Said his father, "Son, where you see nothing there dwells a mighty tree."

[624] What would you do if you learned that you would die tomorrow? Probably you'd abandon all plans for the future; that would be bad. But perhaps you would settle all your old grudges, debts, and favors; that would be good. An old man was planting an apple tree when someone came and said to him, "You may die tomorrow and never see that tree grow up. What about that?" The old man answered, "I would still plant the apple tree."

WITNESSING

[625] Never underestimate your power for good. In your home a tiny candle can prove more useful than the most brilliant star in the sky. In your kitchen the faucet at the sink is more useful than Niagara Falls would be. Our own small powers, rightly used, are sufficient to accomplish whatever is needed. We don't need the strength of Hercules, the physique of a giant, or the silver tongue of an orator; we do need to make the best possible use of the endowments we have.

[626] A commuter on a suburban railroad was known to every regular rider on the 5:15 local. He was a well-dressed, quiet young man. As the train pulled out of the station, he would go to the front of the car in which he was riding and walk down the aisle, speaking to each seatload of passengers as he went. "Excuse me, but if any of your family or friends are blind or threatened with blindness, tell them to consult Dr. Carl. He restored my sight." It was courteous, confident, and courageous testimony, repeated faithfully. The man had good news, and he shared it. This is evangelism!

[627] A group of delegates at a convention was delighted to find that there were no sessions on Sunday. "Let's all go out for a good time," they said. One man held back, saying, "Don't count

on me in your plans. My custom is to worship on Sunday, and that comes first." The rest of the crowd laughed as the word spread: "That poor duck says it's Sunday, so he has to go to church." But later another person broke away from the crowd and said, "I hear you're going to church. I'll come, too." There was a third and a fourth, and finally a good-sized group set off for church, chiefly because of one man's confession.

[628] In 1943 General and Mme. Chiang Kai-shek, the rulers of China and allies of the United States in the war effort, took a full-page advertisement in the *New York Times* headed, "I Bear My Witness." It said in part, "The greatness and love of Christ burst upon me with a new inspiration, increasing my strength to struggle against evil, to overcome temptation and to uphold righteousness. . . . When Christ entered Jerusalem the last time he knew the danger ahead, but triumphantly he rode into the city without fear. What greatness! What courage! In comparison, how unimportant my life must be! Today I have become a follower of Jesus Christ. This is because I realize that we must not sacrifice principle for personal safety under circumstances of difficulty and crisis. In other words, a man's life may be sacrificed or his body held in bondage, but his faith and spirit can never be restrained."

[629] We cannot know from the outside how much water is in a big tank or boiler. However, somewhere on the tank there is usually a tiny glass gauge, and by the amount of water in that gauge we can tell how full the boiler is. If the boiler is empty, the gauge is empty, too.

Love for other people is a kind of gauge of our spiritual life. We cannot tell how much a person loves God, nor should we attempt to judge others. But if a person says, "How do I know how much I love God?" the gauge that may give the answer is, "How much do you love your neighbors?"

[630] Bishop Hugh Latimer was a leader in England's Reformation and an advocate of religious freedom. When the Roman Catholic Queen Mary came into power, Latimer was condemned as a heretic and sentenced to be burned at the stake. As the fire was lighted

around him, he said, "We shall this day light such a candle in England, by God's grace, as I trust shall never be put out."

WORDS

[631] No one questions the power of words today. The whole world is bewitched by them—"bewitched, bothered and bewildered," to quote an old song. A torrent of words pours from the printing press, radio, television, and from every political platform and every soap box. Words move people to buy, sell, hate, and love. They can depress, distort, discourage, and deceive, poisoning the very springs of life. That's why we need to be so careful about what we hear and what we say.

But words can also create new thoughts and arouse courage, faith, and love. Such words are a great power for good. An unexpected word of kindness can change a life and set it on its feet again. A lovely girl in perplexity and trouble discovered that. A little six-year-old boy said to her, "I think you're as beautiful as a fairy princess." She was first embarrassed, then flattered, but finally lifted up out of her mood of depression. A proverb says, "Good advice may fall on barren ground, but a kind word is never thrown away."

[632] Most friends of truth love it as Frederick the Great loved music. It used to be said of him that, strictly speaking, he was not fond of music but of the flute, and not indeed fond of the flute but rather of *his* flute.
RENÉ VINET

[633] The realist says this is a world of material things, hard facts, reason, and common sense. The idealist says it's a world of ideas, imagination, vision, and faith. There's conflict between them because each believes he has spoken a wise word; and actually each has. This is a world of both realities and ideals, and if it's the right kind of place the ideal will be made real.

[634] Oliver Wendell Holmes found one of his patients reading up on diseases. "Careful!" warned Holmes. "Some day you may die of a misprint."

[635] The number 40 appears frequently in religious tradition. Moses led the Israelites through the wilderness for 40 years; the flood resulted from 40 days' rain; Jesus spent 40 days in the wilderness battling temptation by the devil. The number 40 seemed to have some magical cleansing power, or at least some occult significance. Christians set 40 days as the period for Lenten devotion and fasting. Medieval health authorities required incoming vessels to stay offshore for 40 days during time of plague or epidemic before discharging their passengers. From this we get our word *quarantine,* which means a period of 40 days.

[636] Only when the theoretical becomes practical do we have a full understanding of its meaning. You can talk about love and analyze love, but only when you actually love someone does it become concrete and real in your devotion, kindliness, and helpfulness. A kiss is defined as "the anatomical juxtaposition of two orbicular muscles in a state of contraction," but that hardly helps you know the full meaning of a kiss!

[637] Political viewpoints were cleverly defined by President Franklin Delano Roosevelt. He said that if a tree develops rot and begins to decay, the radical says, "Cut it down." The conservative says, "Let it alone." The liberal says, "Prune it and clean it, leaving the good branches and trunk intact." F.D.R. considered himself a liberal, but, by his definition, so must most of us.

[638] The word *church* has a variety of meanings that are often confusing. A Christian creed expresses belief in "one holy, catholic, and apostolic church," but this broad view is not usually evident in the thinking of individuals. For many people, *church* means a building on a street corner. For others, *church* means a congregation, an assortment of people. Still others define *church* as a denomination. Fortunately a few have a broader vision. They define *church* not as a small, ingrown group who like one another's company or as a divided segment with a label slapped on it, but rather as the universal company of believers in Christ.

WORLD AFFAIRS

[639] The world is such a collection of human mistakes and selfishness that some people despair of ever restoring peace and purity to mankind. We need outside help of some sort to set it right again.

A child one day found his father's watch and took it apart. Soon there were dozens of tiny pieces, screws, wheels, gears. When his father came home, the child could only say tearfully, "I'm sorry, daddy." The father tried to put it together but found it impossible, so he carted the whole mess to a local watchmaker.

The watchmaker shook his head, saying, "It'll take a long time to fix, but leave it with me and I'll try to get it working right again." We are like that child with the watch. We can take the world apart, but we need divine help to put it together again.

[640] No political regime based on oppression or military force lasts very long. The ancient Romans probably lasted longer than most, but even their empire declined and fell. Nations that permit injustice, oppression, or aggression are doomed, because they act contrary to God's insistence that God be put first and the welfare of humanity alongside. Governments and political scientists must see that national and racial distinctions are artificial and temporary, because this is one world—God's world.

[641] A TV panelist talked on about the revolutions going on in the world—cultural, political, economic, religious, social, mechanical. A listener said, "He forgot one—the revolution going on in my head right now. I'm dizzy with so many revolutions that the old bean is spinning!"

[642] A father gave his son a globe to stimulate his interest in geography. The boy kept it on a table near his bed. One night there was a news broadcast about a distant Pacific island, and the father wanted to locate it on the map. He tiptoed into the boy's room, picked up the globe, and started to take it out, when the boy sat up in bed and asked, "What are you going to do with my world?"

The father said later, "That question just about knocked me over. What am I going to do with his world? Not the pasteboard globe, but the world he will live in and die in, blown to bits by a bomb, if somebody doesn't do something right with it and pretty soon!"

[643] We cannot remake the world overnight and probably not in our lifetime, but we can do something. Even if we are irritants to society by proclaiming our ideals, we are making a helpful contribution. An oyster is soft and flabby, but when one irritating grain of sand gets into it, it soon becomes a pearl worth more than one thousand oysters. So in this jellyfish world, people of ideals and convictions constitute the one solid piece, the irritant around which God can build his pearl. Never say, "What's the use?" A grain of sand and a mustard seed are tiny, but they have great power.

[644] Charles Beard said history can be compressed into four proverbs:
1. Whom the gods wish to destroy, they first make mad.
2. The mills of the gods grind slowly, but they grind exceeding small.
3. The bee, as it robs the flower, brings the flower the power to live.
4. When it is darkest, we can see the stars.

WORSHIP

[645] I am a regular churchgoer. I would go for various reasons, even if I did not love it. In the corner of my heart there is a plant called reverence, which needs to be watered about once a week.
OLIVER WENDELL HOLMES

[646] Whenever I go past a church
I stop and pay a visit,
So when I'm finally carried in
The Lord won't say, "Who is it?"

[647] A church bulletin board carried the sermon topic and an invitation. It read:

Do you know what hell is like?
Come and hear our choir!

176

[648] An impressive candlelight service was planned to close a youth conference. Each participant lighted a candle at the altar, then proceeded silently out of the church. Everyone was deeply moved, but as soon as they got outdoors, something went wrong. A wind was blowing, and the candles flickered and went out. They tried to relight them, but there was confusion, and the whole effect of the impressive service was defeated.

Candles in the wind aren't enough. If we go out of church feeling that we have left Christ behind for another week, we have failed in our worship. The light must burn steadily.

[649] Abraham Lincoln was a man of deep faith but not a regular churchgoer. Perhaps one thing that turned him away from church was a rule laid down by a congregation he attended occasionally as a youth. It read, "Any member failing three times to attend church meetings without a just cause shall give offense, and they themselves are liable to be reproved as the church may think proper."

[650] The commission preparing the Lutheran *Service Book and Hymnal* removed one stanza from the eighth-century hymn "All glory, laud, and honor" often used on Palm Sunday. The offending stanza read:

Be thou, O Lord, the rider
And we the little ass,
That to God's Holy City
Together we may pass.

I wonder if any congregation could sing that stanza without at least a chuckle? But then, they sometimes sing, "Take my silver and my gold, not a mite would I withhold" without batting an eyelash!

[651] Rituals and books of worship can sometimes become so involved and esoteric that they actually exclude people from participation. They remind me of the youngster who was taken to church by his parents and who heard the minister announce the hymn. "We'll sing number 519, 'Ten Thousand Times Ten Thousand.'

Number 519," he said. The youngster nudged his father and whispered, "Daddy, do we have to work that out?"

[652] During World War II the Nazis occupied Norway and installed a puppet government headed by Vidkun Quisling, a Norwegian traitor. The Quisling regime imprisoned the Lutheran bishops and ordered that one Lutheran service might be held on Sunday morning, but that congregations should gather in their churches on Sunday afternoon to hear political lectures. The Oslo Cathedral was jammed for the morning religious service, but in the afternoon thousands gathered outside its doors in silent protest while only a handful went inside. Police and German soldiers kept the crowd under guard, but there was no rioting or noise. It was a reverent protest, although the threatening and ominous silence seemed as menacing as bricks and stones. Finally, as if at a signal, someone started to sing and thousands of voices took up the words, "A mighty fortress is our God." Then they sang the Norwegian national anthem, and the crowd dispersed. One observer said it was the "most thrilling example of the moral and spiritual freedom of a nation ever seen."

[653] For 18 years an English rector preached in a country parish to an empty church. He received a stipend to conduct the services even if nobody came. Something was wrong with his religion and his common sense, of course. He was satisfied to go through the forms, but the power wasn't turned on, and he didn't care.

[654] We really worship what we value most. Whatever decides our actions and shapes our desires or ambitions is the true object of our worship. Mahatma Gandhi once said of the Christian nations of the West, "They profess to worship a crucified Christ, but their real gods are wealth and power."

[655] One warm summer Sunday the doors of our little church were left open to catch whatever breezes were blowing. A cat took advantage of the open door and walked in during the sermon, strolling up the center aisle. The preacher had to stop for a minute because the congregation was distracted by the unusual visitor. An

usher chased the cat up the aisle, finally cornered it in the choir stalls, and took it outside. When the congregation had settled down again, the minister commented, "At least that cat has more sense than a lot of people. It knew enough to come to church on Sunday morning."

[656] Sir Rowland Hill is best remembered by history as a postal authority who invented the adhesive postage stamp that is now universally used. He deserves to be remembered also for an invocation he delivered one Sunday when he was called upon to offer the opening prayer at a church service. He said, "O Lord, bless mightily those who are in their places. Give grace to those who are on their way; and have mercy on those who are getting ready to come but never will arrive."

WRITERS AND WRITING

[657] Famed editor George Horace Lorimer told of an indignant author who wrote to him that he had failed to read her entire manuscript. "I pasted pages 16, 17, and 18 together, and you did not separate them," she charged.

Lorimer replied, "Madam, when I eat an egg at breakfast, I do not have to eat the whole thing before I find out whether it is good or bad."

[658] The first requirement in any piece of writing is to attract the reader's attention. Dorothy Parker and Robert Benchley once shared the same office in the old Metropolitan Opera building in New York. Benchley was often away, and Miss Parker was lonesome in the little office. Then she discovered a way to assure all sorts of attention. She painted out the sign on the door that held both their names and instead painted on just one word: Gentlemen. After that she never lacked for visitors!

[659] Long, involved sentences confuse me, and I am obliged to reread them to get the sense. At times I may indulge myself in a long one, but I make sure there are no folds in it, no vagueness, no parenthetical interruptions of its view as a whole; when I am done

with it, it won't be a sea serpent, with half its arches under water; it will be a torchlight procession.

The difference between the almost-right word and the right word is really a large matter. It is the difference between the lightning bug and the lightning.

MARK TWAIN

[660] For a writer, experience is necessary. Books are not bred by a sort of immaculate conception, but by people and life in constant and abrasive interconnection. The study of forms, important though it is, is not as important as having something to say. People like Yeats, Kipling, Shaw, and Lawrence had little formal education to learn to write, but they had vast experience. Melville's Harvard and Yale was a whaling ship. What makes literature great is the quality of its subject matter.

[661] Nobody would be likely to give a piano recital or offer to translate Mark Twain into Russian without having some background of study and practice to make such an offer valid. The concert pianist spends years in the misery of scales and etudes and exercises before he can perform. The language scholar spends endless time learning idiom, conjugation, vocabulary, and all the rest before claiming to be a skillful translator. But writers? Oh, anybody can write! It no longer surprises me when someone offers to write a novel, adding that a generous advance payment would be acceptable. Then I ask, "What have you written? Let's see samples of your work." Often the answer is, "Oh, I haven't written much yet—at least nothing that's published. But I've got this great idea, see, and if you'll publish it I'll get right to work."

Index of
Sources and Topics

The numbers following each entry refer to illustration numbers, not pages, in the text.

Achilles 81
Adam and Eve 407, 415
Adversity 1-12, 176, 266, 468
Advertising 579, 581, 583, 620
Age 13, 14, 315, 601
Air Travel 534, 604
Alcoholics 588
Ambition 472, 503
Andrews, Roy Chapman 505
Animals 79, 237, 330, 655
Anxiety (see *Worry*) 15-23,
    179, 194, 354, 429
Archaeology 52
Architecture 431
Armies 562
Art and Artists 24-31, 94, 132,
    156, 159, 168, 171, 260, 272,
    363, 364, 556, 614
Atheists 150, 152, 255
Attendance, Church (see
    Worship) 187, 190, 191,
    292, 359, 496, 546, 627
Attitude 32-39, 144, 145, 215,
    289, 365, 413, 456, 497
Augustine 141, 205

Beauty 34, 341, 342
Beecher, Henry Ward 19, 21,
    497, 581

Bible 6, 40-53, 89, 95, 149,
    451, 539, 549
Birthdays 13, 607
Bishops 213
Blessings 595, 620
Books 54-56
Brashear, John 336
Brotherhood 57-68, 106, 133,
    180, 185, 328, 352, 611
Browne, Thomas 201
Bunyan, John 200
Burns, Robert 325
Burrell, D. James 346
Bushnell, Horace 167
Bystanders 348

Camping 406
Candles 648
Carlyle, Thomas 55, 59, 137
Carver, George Washington
    122
Challenge 7, 82, 146, 161,
    220, 246
Change 69-72, 157, 217, 256,
    532, 536, 600, 601
Character 73-83, 112, 117,
    183, 215, 367
Charity 84, 85, 213, 569, 598
Children 12, 22, 36, 72, 86,

87, 110, 208, 277, 291, 322
385, 406, 416
China   367, 463, 628
Christianity   88-95, 165
Christmas   96-108, 371
Churches   109-116, 160, 187,
216, 638
Clocks   526, 606
Commandments   555
Coffin, Henry Sloane   514
Commitment   117-126, 161,
163, 187, 247, 249, 284,
362, 424
Commager, Henry S.   435
Communications   127, 128, 361
Communism   280
Compassion   129-133, 172, 213,
253, 420
Competition   57, 125, 147, 365
Composers   80
Compton, Arthur H.   507
Conflict   18, 72, 115, 149, 354,
508
Conscience   134-137, 172, 366,
438, 643
Constitution, U.S.   50, 232, 444
Contentment   138-144, 297,
316, 317, 514, 596
Courage   145-148, 241, 552, 618
Creation   149-154
Cross   155-160, 371, 511

Death   (see *Immortality*)   324,
335, 646
Decision   161-170, 188, 224,
237, 373
Depth   44

Despair   320, 321
Determination   75, 147, 221,
249, 448, 453
Devil   305
Discovery, Age of   70, 447
Disputes, Church   2, 57, 110,
115, 116, 232, 368
Disunity   57, 58, 114, 610
Doors   511
Dow, Willard H.   537
Downey, Fairfax   594
Drummond, Henry   91

Easter   342, 353
Ecumenism   114, 191, 610
Editors   659
Education   43, 404, 660
Edwards, Jonathan   2
Einstein, Albert   153, 216
Elgar, Edward   80
Elizabeth 1   499
Emerson, Ralph Waldo   450
Episcopalians   110, 183
Epistles   42
Equality   258, 427, 446
Erdman, Walter   83
Everyday Religion   171-185,
274, 476, 512, 597, 648
Evil   78, 391
Example   359, 361, 395, 436,
550
Excuses   190, 191, 348, 548
Experience   660, 661

Failure   9, 12, 372, 400
Faith   (see *Trust*)   74, 192-212,
280, 299, 305

Faith at Work   182, 213-220
Faithfulness,   (see *Loyalty*)
    187, 188, 221-224, 376, 378,
    379, 402, 462
False Hopes   225-227, 228, 473
Family   (see *Marriage*) 343,
    360
Farmers   74, 84, 176, 250, 457,
    459, 617
Fathers   91, 271, 275, 414, 420
Fear   17, 145, 191, 233, 239,
    303, 392, 533
Fearing, Kenneth   429
Fletcher, John   266
Flowers   1, 378
Forgetfulness   522, 523
Forgiveness   24, 136, 137, 231,
    251, 303-311, 326
Franklin, Benjamin   261, 345,
    355, 444
Freedom   228-237, 350, 652
Friendship   64, 68
Fry, Franklin Clark   407
Future   238-242, 245, 346, 386,
    513, 602, 624

Gandhi   126, 481, 654
Gardens   (see *Nature*) 242-
    245, 337, 622
Gardner, John W.   347
Garfield, James   125
Giving   97, 100, 101, 102, 104,
    117, 370, 565, 567, 569, 574
Goals   246-249, 500, 541, 543
God's Love   250-258, 306, 358
God's Power   259-270, 528

God's Presence   271-281, 356,
    421, 477, 478
God's Promises   282-285, 480
Goethe, Johann Wolfgang von
    155, 207
Graciousness   39, 49, 525
Gray, Horace   390
Greed   286-291, 314
Growth   292-294, 447, 510
Guidance   89, 198, 209, 295-
    302
Guilt   136, 303-311, 348, 390
Gustavus Adolphus   161

Halloween   271
Handicaps   147, 596, 615
Happiness   312-317, 471, 541
Hawthorne, Nathaniel   129
Health   73, 626, 634, 635
Heroes   186, 530
Heyer, "Father"   424
History, Lessons of   8, 70, 109,
    174, 223, 241, 438, 644
Holmes, Oliver Wendell   595,
    634
Home   428, 603
Hope   245, 318-324, 341, 344,
    364, 621
Hough, Lynn Harold   362
Hugo, Victor   213
Humility   32, 148, 270, 301,
    304, 325-335, 490, 537
Humor   42, 51, 380-385, 491,
    493, 604, 647
Hurst, Fannie   593
Huxley, Aldous   538

Hypocrisy   67, 214, 412, 508,
    519, 562

Idealism   120, 633, 643
Idols   51
Imagination   616, 617, 623
Immortality   55, 90, 281,
    336-346
Indians   66
Indifference   178, 179, 347-353,
    433, 515
Individuals   354-358, 549
Influence   359-364, 397, 527
Insight   93, 107, 129, 281, 298,
    585
Integrity   365-379

Jeans, Sir James   154
Judgment   129, 390, 649
Justice   418, 427

Kempis, Thomas à   466
Kierkegaard, Søren   276
Kindness   181, 185, 547
Kingsley, Charles   228
Kiss   636
Knowledge   243, 259, 279,
    333, 368
Kreisler, Fritz   426

Labor   366, 376, 378, 379,
    386-388
Lamps   41, 189
Lateness   385, 656
Law   234, 235, 328, 389-392

Lawmakers   32
Lee, Robert E.   396
Leonardo da Vinci   24, 27, 132
Light   41, 47, 298, 300, 302,
    431, 587
Lincoln, Abraham   162, 649
Lippman, Walter   391
Literature   28
Livingstone, David   278
Lord's Supper   85
Love   (see God's Love)
    393-395
Loyalty   396-401
Luther, Martin   5, 36, 142,
    143, 144, 169, 177, 195,
    229, 230, 262, 264, 305,
    320, 492, 494, 529, 590
Lutherans   113, 427, 650

Malachi   282
Maltby, W. R.   285
Marriage   402-416
Measures   629
Menninger, Karl   394
Mercy   417-420
Michelangelo   30, 363, 378
Mirrors   29, 327, 395
Missions   421-427
Modern Art   25
Modern Life   428-435, 438,
    500, 505, 533, 534, 536
Moffatt, James   513
Money   283, 290, 373, 375,
    432, 567, 570
Moody, Dwight L.   356
Morality   403, 430
Morley, Christopher   226, 582

Morrison, A. Cressy   151
Mothers   439-443
Music   80, 326, 426, 613, 647

Names   33, 124
Napoleon   263, 399, 418
National   50, 398, 444-446,
    507, 519
Nature   1, 3, 65, 72, 142, 143,
    235, 242, 243, 259, 317,
    392, 561
Neighbors   59, 85, 352
Netherlands   265
Newton, Isaac   150
Newton, John   560
New Year   600
Nightingale, Florence   423
Nimitz, Chester W.   446
Norway   652
Numbers   635, 651

Obedience   425, 441, 555
Opportunity   447-459, 542, 625
Oxenham, John   597

Parables   586
Parkhurst, Charles H.   411
Patience   255, 429, 453, 460-
    463
Patmore, Coventry   420
Patriotism   50, 396, 398
Peace   62, 119, 120, 140, 303,
    464-469
Persecution   60, 109, 113, 148,
    216, 630
Perseverance   479

Personality   (see *Character*)
Physicians   119, 123, 422
Pledging   121, 124, 573, 574
Political parties   637, 640
Popularity   558
Poverty   4
Power   (see *God's Power*)   40,
    48, 83, 164, 387, 470-474,
    528, 561, 631
Prayer   374, 380, 417, 475-489,
    491
Preaching   361, 460, 490-497,
    610
Prejudice   37, 65, 110, 461, 524
Presbyterians   110, 122
Pride   498, 499
Priorities   82, 139, 248, 286,
    288, 428
Progress   500-506
Promises   (see *God's Promises*)
    200, 203, 282-285
Protection   271, 437, 465, 554
Prudence   568, 569
Purim, Feast of   60

Rainbow   318
Reading   43, 45
Reagan, Ronald   170
Rebirth   77, 169, 217, 218,
    268, 612
Refugees   86, 87
Religion, Personal   (see
    Everyday Religion)   99,
    103, 105, 107, 126, 165, 166,
    174, 254, 423
Remembrance   521-525
Repetition   72

186

Resources, Inner 526-529
Revolutions 641
Rewards 530-531
Ritual 651, 653
Roman Catholics 213, 408,
    469, 518, 611
Roosevelt, Franklin Delano
    637

Sacrifice 66, 97, 100, 119, 122,
    222, 250, 278, 284, 398, 439
Salt 437
Scherer, Paul 164
School 36, 277
Science 1, 128, 241, 330,
    532-539
Science and Religion 52, 150,
    151, 152, 153, 279, 471,
    489, 505, 509, 535, 537
Secularism 96, 103, 108, 175,
    199, 375, 517
Self-righteousness 67, 219,
    233, 329, 332, 389, 578
Service 540-548
Shaheen, E. Raymond 516
Shakespeare 419, 490
Shangri-La 69
Sharing 61, 63, 68, 240, 291,
    313, 525
Shaw, George Bernard 88
Sheen, Fulton J. 558
Sheep and Shepherds 549-553
Silence 38, 196, 296, 360
Sin (see Evil) 554-561, 592
Socrates 118, 409
Space 532, 535

Speakers 381, 382, 383, 493,
    495
Sports 365, 397
Spurgeon, Charles Haddon
    91, 204, 256
Stars 334, 336, 532
Statues 31
Steinmetz, Charles P. 471
Stewardship 282, 288, 294,
    310, 366, 370, 379, 451,
    531, 562-578
Strength, Spiritual 11, 48, 145
Success 579-583
Suffering 5, 129, 131, 278
Sunday, 92, 434, 476, 627
Sunday School 46, 166
Superstition 225, 334
Suspicion 39, 407
Swift, Jonathan 506

Talmud 458
Teachers 363, 440, 584-587
Television 127
Temptation 588-592
Tennyson, Alfred 496
Thanksgiving 593-599
Thoreau, Henry 503
Time 526, 572, 600-608
Tolstoi 185, 388
Towne, Charles Hanson 196
Travel 75, 77, 293, 295, 299,
    534, 572, 591, 604
Trees 245
Trinity 267
Trust (see Faith) 262, 269,
    273, 369

Twain, Mark 659
Tyndale, William 6

Unbelief 150, 198, 210
Unity 609-613

Values 26, 28, 127, 227, 289,
    290, 294, 312, 365, 430,
    452, 501, 566
Velikovsky, Immanuel 539
Vinet, René 632
Vision 289, 293, 319, 341, 355,
    614-624

Wallace, Henry 464
Walton, Izaak 522
Wanamaker, John 134, 495
Washington, George 445
Weakness 20, 81
Wealth 4, 139, 199, 227, 286

Webster, Daniel 460, 462
Wesley, John 308, 527, 580
Wilder, Thornton 343
Wilson, Woodrow 120
Witnessing 625-630
Wives 42, 402, 403, 410
Wood, Eugene 315
Woollcott, Alexander 138
Words 631-638, 659
World Affairs 86, 88, 120, 148,
    158, 202, 240, 464, 473, 509,
    540, 639-644
Worry (see *Anxiety*) 46, 142,
    143, 314, 467
Worship 645-656
Writers 657-661

Yorktown, Battle of 398
Youthfulness 14

Zwingli, Ulrich 214